LUCKY DIP

Catharine Boddy was born in Norfolk, and now lives in Scarborough, where she works as a teacher. Her poems have appeared in *loads* of books before now, but this is the first one she's had all to herself...

To Emily
Enjoy these poems
and keep collecting
words.
Catharine
Boddy.

Lucky Dip

poems by
Catharine Boddy

with illustrations by
John Taylor

Valley Press

First published in 2016 by Valley Press
Woodend, The Crescent, Scarborough, YO11 2PW
www.valleypressuk.com

First edition, first printing (September 2016)

ISBN 978-1-908853-79-0
Cat. no. VP0096

Poems copyright © Catharine Boddy 2016
Illustrations copyright © John Taylor 2016

The right of Catharine Boddy to be identified as the author of this work has been asserted in accordance with the Copyright, Designs and Patents Act 1988.

All rights reserved. No part of this publication may be reproduced, stored in or introduced into a retrieval system, or transmitted in any form, by any means (electronic, mechanical, photocopying, recording or otherwise) without prior written permission from the rights holders.

A CIP record for this book is available from the British Library.

Printed and bound in Great Britain by
Charlesworth Press, Wakefield

Contents

Dragon 9
What it takes to be a good friend 10
Excuses Excuses 11
Spinner 13
A tasty family 14
Ancient oak 15
A night to remember 16
Silent friend 20
Puzzled 21
Urban fox 23
One man team 24
Ball skills 26
A little problem 27
An early visitor 29
My teeth? 30
Mum is… 31
Don't you dare 33
School dinner, nothing grimmer 34
Seaside setting 35
Night 36

For Laura.

Always dare to dream.

Dragon

A dragon lives beneath Mum's bed.
I know it does but my Mum said
it's daft to say something like that –
we haven't even got a cat!

But I sneaked in there late at night
and gave myself a nasty fright.
Little puffs of smoke were seen
gliding upwards, bright pea green.

I pressed myself against the door
as strong claws scraped across the floor.
One rumble was enough for me,
I dared not have a look to see

if Mum had got herself a pet.
I'd really like to know, and yet
why does she feel she cannot share
the creature that she keeps in there?

Of course, it might outgrow the bed.
Then will she keep it in the shed?
The thing that's really bothering me
is something that my Mum can't see –

she jokes and smiles and pulls my leg,
but where'd she get a dragon egg?

What it takes to be a good friend

Great mate
Talk straight
Gossip bearer
Trouble sharer
Staunch defender
Text sender
Town shopper
Clothes swapper
Tear drier
Present buyer
Party thrower
Secrets knower
Best friends forever
Fall out? Never!

Excuses Excuses

He plots in the early dawn:
I can't go to school Mum.
My head aches.
I feel sick.
Don't make me go.

He rehearses as the day breaks:
I can't go to school Mum.
I've lost my P.E. kit.
I haven't done my homework.
Don't make me go.

He pleads over breakfast:
I can't go to school Mum.
My stomach hurts.
You don't understand.
Don't make me go.

As she turns away,
he whispers...
They'll be waiting for me.

Spinner

Eight legs,
lots of eyes,
sticky spinner
catches flies.
Scuttles quickly
up the walls,
shoots his web
and down he falls.
In the bathroom,
under chairs,
spiders can
live anywhere.
We think them hairy,
call them scary,
but in England
they don't bite
and early in the morning
their lovely webs
drip light.

A tasty family

My brother has a hamster.
My granny has a rat.
My sister has a guinea pig
that sleeps in a top hat.
My dad looks after gerbils.
My mum, she likes her mouse.
Me, I have a rabbit that
roams around the house.

The problem is my cousin,
an evil lad named Jake;
when he comes to visit us
he always brings his snake.
We have to hide our furry friends
because (this is the crunch)
Jake's lovely hungry python
thinks all our pets are lunch!

Ancient oak

Leaves whisper,
turn gold,
another year is growing old.
Still you stand.

Bare branches,
roots deep,
slumber in your winter sleep.
Still you stand.

Spring buds,
life teems,
in all your wrinkles, nooks and seams.
Still you stand.

Summer light,
carved face,
powerful in this time and place.
Still you stand.

Seasons pass,
time flies,
ancient oak tree, tall and wise,
the watcher in the woods
still stands.

A night to remember

*'Twas the night before Christmas,
when all through the house
not a creature was stirring,
not even a mouse...*

That is the start of
a very old poem,
but I'm sorry to say
quite untrue of my home.

'Twas the night before Christmas
and oh, by the way,
'twas the night at the end of
a very long day.

On Christmas Eve morning
the snow was quite deep,
great fun for us
but Gran walks in her sleep.

We found her outside
looking rather confused
with snow on her hairnet
and toes turning blue.

We then built a big snowman
all gleaming and bright,
but my brother destroyed it
so we had a fight.

My poor mother stared
and said 'Well! What a mess!
But the black eye will go with
your new party dress.'

We put up the trimmings
and finished the tree.
Though I say it myself
it was lovely to see.

Unfortunately we had
forgotten the cat,
who mistook our tree fairy
for a mouse or a rat.

The tree then fell into
our Dad's favourite chair
(but no-one had noticed
that Grandpa was there).

And so off to bed
at the end of the day
but my brother had something
he wanted to say.

'I've put out this note
for Santa to see,'
he said, waving an old
scrap of paper at me.

*I don't want a skateboard
or new games to play,
I want Santa to please
take my sister away!*

I ask for a Christmas
of goodwill and peace;
or maybe a truce
that will last till next week?

Silent friend

You always listen carefully.
You always take my part.
You never interrupt me.
You know what's in my heart.
You never hurt my feelings.
You're always keen to play.
You know just when to hug me.
and when to stay away.
You can make me happy.
You never make me sad.
(But when you chew my mobile phone
it really makes me mad!)
I love you in the morning.
I love you late at night.
You're absolutely 'girl's best friend'.
We've never had a fight.
So go and fetch your lead, dog.
It's time to have a walk.
I think we'll be gone quite a while.
We need to have a talk!

Puzzled

Our jigsaw is incomplete.
We've lost a piece and
it will never be the same again.
It *was* whole.
We fitted together well.
Together we were strong.
But now my mum and I
must fit together as best we can
around the gap,
although there will always be
a piece missing.

Urban fox

Fox, slink through the dark.
What are you looking for?
Fox, slide through the dark
close to my back door.

Fox, lurk in the shadows
watching all that moves.
Fox, hide in the shadows
searching for some food.

Fox, in the town at night
raiding people's bins.
Fox saw the people –
did anyone see him?

One man team

'Why don't you stick it in the net?'
the angry goalie cried.
'We've not come for a picnic,
but to beat the other side!'

Baz is looking dozy
(sadly nothing new),
Kevin seems to have a limp,
and John-o wants the loo.

Darren's shorts are slipping
(hope he keeps them up),
Mr Frost can't bear to look,
he's praying for some luck.

'You'll need more than good fortune,'
said Baz's brother Dean.
'Yes,' agreed our poor old Head,
'we need a brand new team!'

A gasp rose from the balcony,
then silence filled the hall.
Our goalie'd left his area,
gone dribbling with the ball.

He weaved through opposition
and team members alike.
At last, before the other goal,
our keeper poised to strike.

His boot connected with the ball,
it made a graceful flight
into the corner of the net –
a quite amazing sight.

Calmly dusting off his hands
he walked past all the dads,
then turning, shouted to his mates:
'That's how you do it lads!'

Ball skills

They said he'd help us win the cup.
They said he was the best.
They said we ought to buy him,
in him we should invest.

So we gave him a trial...

He could kick it,
he could flick it,
he could bounce it on his knee.
He could flip it,
he could chip it,
he'd do tricks for all to see.
He could twirl it on his finger,
make it spin around his head,

but he couldn't score for toffee
so we kicked him out instead!

A little problem

A poem to read to parents at the check-in desk!

Mum, I've something to tell you
as we stand here in this queue.
I should have said this yesterday,
I'm not sure what to do.
I was looking at my passport,
I thought I'd have a laugh,
but it wasn't very funny
when I dropped it in the bath!
I put it in the microwave
to try to dry it out
before I put it in my case –
Mum, promise you won't shout.
I really meant to pick it up
but you know I got up late
then forgot to pack my iPad;
I was really in a state.
So I thought I ought to mention it,
I thought you ought to know,
because *without* my passport
I don't think we can go…

today… anyway…

An early visitor

A dinosaur came to breakfast.
He ate all of the toast,
he ate all of the cereal –
in fact, he ate the most!

He loved the eggs and bacon,
he cleared the porridge pot,
he hoovered up the kippers –
in truth, he ate the lot.

He thanked my mum politely.
He carefully wiped his claws.
He flicked his tail round neatly
and lumbered out the door.

We've stocked up at the market
on fruit and fish and peas,
on bread, potatoes, rice and meat
in case he comes to tea…

My teeth?

Of course they're clean Mum,
I scrubbed them well last night.
Must I do them now, this morning,
to keep them dazzling white?
Well I'll just put my shoes on,
and I'll just feed the cat
and get the knots out of my hair,
I'll do them after that.
Of course I'll clean my teeth Mum.
I want them to be nice,
sparkling like the adverts
and fresh as winter ice...
but I'll just find my homework
and I've lost my P.E. skirt,
there's paint on my grey trousers
and I need a clean school shirt.
What? My teeth? All right Mum!
I'm getting out my brush.
Honestly, I do not know
why there's all this fuss!

Mum is...

Rule maker
Side taker
Meal provider
Bedroom tidier
Game player
Bug slayer
Story teller
Homework helper
Peace keeper
Light sleeper
Money lender
Chief defender

Loves her child
However wild!

Don't you dare

Don't say no to a dinner lady.
Don't even shake your head,
as she stands armed with a ladle
and you want to be fed.

Don't say no to a dinner lady
if she says 'peas, not beans'.
She's had special training
to make you eat your greens.

Don't say no to a dinner lady
when she says 'fruit today'.
If you don't eat that apple
you won't go out to play.

Don't say no to a dinner lady.
Eat your meat and fish.
Don't ever ask for junk food,
clean every plate and dish.

Don't say no to a dinner lady.
Don't have any doubts –
if you say no to a dinner lady
she'll only give you *sprouts*.

School dinner, nothing grimmer

Meat as tough as leather shoes
or something odd that they call stew,
all served up with gruesome greens,
peas and cabbage, stringy beans,
mashed potatoes, loads of lumps,
gravy with suspicious bumps,
pink sponge cake as heavy as lead,
custard you could slice like bread,
fruit that is a few weeks old –
fine, if you scrape off the mould.
All guaranteed to make you thinner.
Diet? No, just try school dinners!

Seaside setting

I love it at the seaside
when the crowds have all gone home,
when there's only me and sand and sky
and loads of space to roam.

I love it at the seaside
when the dark clouds gather round,
when the wind whips up white horses
that crash and splash and pound.

I love it at the seaside
when the crowds have gone away –
when winter means an empty beach,
that's when I want to stay.

Night

You sleep…
but outside, an owl hunts on silent wings,
a fox scavenges in your bins,
a badger feeds and roams around,
rabbits emerge from underground,
rats scratch and breed and fight,
cats meet when the moon is bright.

And you sleep…
but nurses work to treat and heal,
tired doctors eat a hasty meal,
factory workers start their shifts,
taxi drivers give late lifts,
babies can't wait to be born,
others die and families mourn,

and you sleep on until the dawn.

NORFOLK AU...
SAMUEL J WHITE

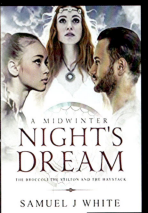

SET IN CROMER NORFOLK
A book like nothing you have read before. In the strangest of situations. Naked and cold, Strangers Rob and Kat are entwined together both physically and through a series of shared dreams as they try to keep each other warm after a bizarre incident. Flashing between a deadly situation in the present and heartwarming dreams of the future. They must figure out what's really going on before it's too late. A twisting romantic mystery with comedy and tragedy, ghosts and angels. A story to give hope to anyone who is lonely.

"This author needs to be picked up by a big publisher. This story was emotionally turbulent. I laughed so hard I cried and cried so hard I had to blow my nose. I can't wait to read his other books!!!" Review Keri Kankovsky USA

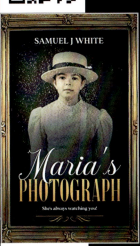

Based on a true story about a Photograph in the school in Hevingham Norfolk.
After being widowed in the second world war, Young School teacher Judith moves to start a new life in a remote Norfolk village. Finding herself alone in her remote cottage for long evenings she often finds herself talking to an old photograph of a young girl which came with the house. When the girl begins to haunt her dreams Judith becomes involved in a terrifying and jumpy ghost story.

"MARIA'S PHOTOGRAPH IS CREEPY, GRIPPING, SURPRISINGLY LOVING, AND DIFFICULT TO PUT DOWN.
IT IS ONE OF THOSE BOOKS THAT TAKES HOLD OF YOU AND MAKES YOU THINK YOU KNOW HOW THINGS ARE GOING TO GO, BUT YOU ARE OH SO WRONG.
SAMUEL J WHITE HAS WOVEN A MASTERFUL TALE AND DOESN'T LEAVE YOU DISAPPOINTED."
REVIEW BY AUTHOR RICHARD GRIFFITH USA

SCAN THE QR CODES TO GET LINKS TO EBOOKS AND MORE REVIEWS

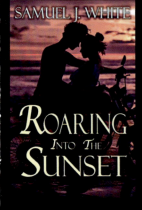

Set in 1980/90s Norwich In the split second before they feel the impact of their possible impending doom. The lives of the adrenaline junky couple Dave and Sarah flash before their eyes. But after all their struggles will their lives end this way? Or can they stop it? A twisting, warming, humourous, yet heartwrenching, coming-of-age tale. Told by both Dave and Sarah set against the backdrop of the '80s and 90s East Anglia. (Some scenes have themes of violence and attitudes which belong in the past.)

"The author takes his readers on an interesting and wonderful journey with the main characters in such a way it feels as though you know them personally. I enjoyed this novel immensely. I would highly recommend this literary masterpiece to anyone and everyone. " Tenesha Miller

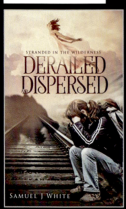

Set on the railway between Norwich and Great Yarmouth. Ongoing series (Currently four volumes) The Survivors of a train crash in the marshes go to get help only to find that Acle Straight road has vanished and there's a great evil waiting in the darkness. Adventure with witches, vampires and werewolves.

"The tension and horror builds slowly, catching the reader by surprise. Prepare yourself for plot twists and surprises-there's even a dash of romance. Might wanna make sure the electric bill is paid up as you'll want to sleep with the lights on for a while." Pia Manning

Add me on facebook Author Samuel J White

Facebook

Newsletter sign up

Website
https://samjwhite9.wixsite.com/samuel-j-white-books

Derailed and dispersed
Volume 2

The evil in the darkness

Samuel J White

[signature]
25/8/2024

SJW Publishing

Copyright © [2019] by [Samuel J White]

All rights reserved.

No portion of this book may be reproduced in any form without written permission from the publisher or author, except as permitted by U.K. and US copyright law.

Edited by Ann Atwood

Contents

1. Chapter 1 WRITTEN IN MAY 2019 JESSICA — 1
2. Chapter 2 GEORGIE – PART 2.1 — 5
3. Chapter 3 JAMES — 15
4. Chapter 4 Rachel — 23
5. Chapter 5 Charlie — 32
6. Chapter 6 Mandy — 42
7. Chapter 7 Sadie — 51
8. Chapter 8 Jenny — 56
9. Chapter 9 Jessica — 60
10. Chapter 10 Becky — 70
11. Chapter 11 Georgie — 79
12. Chapter 11 Sharon — 87
13. Chapter 12 Amber — 92
14. Chapter 14 Sharon — 100
15. Derailed and Dispersed Volume 3 is out now — 104

Chapter 1 WRITTEN IN MAY 2019 JESSICA

Dear reader, thank you for taking the time to pick up the second part of our story. My friends and colleagues and I have agreed to continue telling our story in bite-sized chunks. I don't want to bore people by going over what happened in Part One so if you haven't read it then it's best you do.

Although J&M Enterprises continued to work in the weeks, months and years following the events of the 22nd of December 1999, the line-up of staff was never quite the same.

Some of the staff, including people who have written in this book, never returned to door-to-door sales. However, I am proud to say that after we diversified the company, many of those people work for J&M in another capacity, or like Amber they run a business which we own. We now have investments in many different places, J&M Enterprises now includes a letting agency, many pubs and several gyms as well as the sales department.

On top of this Mandy and I run a section of the business where we help young people who are in the situation we were in. We go into schools and colleges one day a week and give advice.

Enough about the business, we were supposed to be writing this piece together like before, but I know that others have already started. It's the final days of May, the sun has gone down and the kids are sleeping, but I'm home with the kids on my own. My husband has gone away on a business trip. With the money I earn, my husband doesn't need to work, but he's his own person and earns a great deal in his own right and can easily say the same about me.

He hates going and leaving me and the kids because he loves us all so much, as we do him. Usually, if he can, he only stays away for one night, if that, and when he can he'll be back in one day. He left at four o'clock for a conference in Northern Ireland this morning and was supposed to be flying back this evening.

I was going to meet him at the station with the kids.

However, late this afternoon I saw that all British Airways flights had been cancelled because of a computer problem. I wish his boss had listened when we told him it was much more cost-effective to use budget airlines.

Well, with two young kids who are upset that Daddy isn't coming home, and a baby who's teething, you'd think I'd be glad to use whatever spare time I have to sleep. But I don't sleep when he's gone. Since we began to write the story, memories of the past still reap terror in my brain.

Some years ago, we purchased a house in Halvegate, a small village on the western side of the marsh. My office is in the attic at the rear of the house and has a window that faces three directions, so I can look out over the marsh. It's so vast that even if you look out of the attic window in broad daylight you can just about see the railway, but you need binoculars to see the place where the train crashed. I keep my binoculars close at all times. People think I'm mad, and maybe I am. There are CCTV cameras all around the house. Why do I live somewhere so close to where it happened if I wanted to protect my family from it? I often feel it's good to keep friends close... and your demons closer.

I look at my children sleeping as the wind batters this creepy house and wonder what kind of a world my children will grow up in. Unlike many others, my children will be fed, clothed, educated and want for nothing. That, however, doesn't stop me from worrying about their future.

Every night I see the monsters in my dreams, smiles on their faces and blood of a million people on their hands, laughing. Then I wake up and realise I have fallen asleep watching a recording of Prime Minister's Questions and pray to God that this evil government is not re-elected. That's because I know who is really behind all their wrongdoings. I always get up and check all of the windows and doors before staying awake for at least another hour before I can sleep again, if at all. That's not hard when you have insomnia.

So, with my husband away there will be no sleep tonight. The sun has said its long goodbye, and the pale sad moon is not even close to full. I'm okay, I kid myself as I kiss my baby daughter's head.

I don't know what I would do if I did see something out of the ordinary. I can always call the Police, but what help would that be? I can imagine their reaction now.

Police: 'How can we be of help, Madam?

Me: 'Well, there are some scary people on the marsh who might be able to do magic. Can you help?'

Police: 'What have you been smoking Madam?'

After the train came off the rails, I was to learn that there is much more evil in the world than we can ever imagine. Every bump or creek in this old house, the howl of the wind or the tapping of the rain on the window makes me shudder. Every time I sneeze, I think it's them causing people to be ill again.

Jenny tells me things now and again. She shuns her people and believes them to be behind the unrest that has gone on in the world over the last few years. I have her on speed dial in my phone, speed being the word, being as she can run at the speed of light, she can fly, and a few other things you probably think I'm shitting you about.

Anyway, enough of my scaremongering and political views. I think the best thing to do would be to summarise what happened in Volume One, then hand the story over to somebody else.

A very brief summary is this. After our train derailed and exploded several people were missing, Kate was in labour and her twin sister Becky had a badly broken leg. Two groups, led by Chris and Sharon, went to search the marsh. Chris's group found Kate's partner, John, dead, while Rob described how Sharon's group were captured by people in masks.

My best friend and co-owner of the company, Mandy, had taken a group down the tracks inland where Irish Sammy--who was drunk—found a dying lady who she believed to be her future self, and Spanish Sadie had been snatched by something in the dark.

I went East along the tracks towards the coast with James, and my long-time friend Charlie, my glasses were broken and I couldn't see properly, and after an asthma attack, I saw the ghost of my dead brother before kissing Charlie. Then James and Charlie both vanished, and in looking for them, I bumped into Mandy and Sadie who should have been miles away in the other direction. With them was Tom the conductor, who seemed to have made an amazing recovery after he was decapitated earlier in the evening.

Georgie and Amber who were both among the missing told of how Amber was taken by a monster.

Georgie also told of her encounter earlier that day with a girl with magical powers. That girl was Jenny who joined our group to tell her story and pretty much frightened the hell out of us.

So rather than start with my own long-winded story I want to hand it over.

Chapter 2 GEORGIE — PART 2.1

For those of you who don't remember me from volume one, I'm the friendly quiet lady with no legs and serious memory problems. I had an encounter with a girl who could read my past and speak to spirits. That was before the train crashed and I was rescued by Amber only to see her dragged away by a monster.

Just to be clear I'm not an angel I do enjoy a glass of wine or beer responsibly. (I should not really drink at all because of my epilepsy meds) But being unsteady on my prosthetics, while others don't drink and drive I don't drink and walk, and certainly don't smoke anything let alone mind-bending drugs.

I was stone-cold sober, and I'm not the biggest fan of swearing but FUCK ME that was some scary thing that took Amber.

People often ask me what I've been doing in the past Twenty or so years. Well…. I inherited a multibillion-pound business. So naturally I retreated to my dark lair and put on a mask and suit and fought bad guys. Oh no, wait sorry I'm confusing myself with Batman again. Both are crazy billionaires I suppose but I've been putting my time and money to better use. All will be revealed soon enough.

After reading what people wrote in volume one. I've addressed some things about me with people. I saw my name used in the same sentences as 'Pretty' and 'Intelligent.' I won't tell people what to think privately but come on guys it's disrespectful to those who really are both of those things and there were others in the group whom the words better describe. I mean for example Rachel, who went on to be a lecturer at the University of EAST ANGLIA. Don't put me on her level it's not fair on her.

Also, I'm flattered that many people admitted to having a crush on me Twenty years ago. You should have told me then and you might have got some action. Mind out of the gutter guys I don't mean sex,

I may have been quietly spoken and looked like a girly girl. I liked pretty things but often went on my own to watch action movies and football. I would have loved some company male or female. Just mates though. You're Twenty years too late though.

The world has changed so much since. Back then because of my memory setbacks, I was still coming out of my social shell. I'm much different to the girl I was back then. Less introverted, more outspoken, opinionated and forceful with my opinions. People tell me that myself and Jessie have similar personalities as we've got older, and I agree with that. Because of my brain injury and lack of direction in my life in the following years, Jessie became my role model and that's why.

My work partner Jimmy lives on in me through my blunt and dry sense of humour, which I may well of got from him. Despite what you're going to learn about Jimmy in the rest of this series of books, he was my friend and a good man and I still miss him despite what he did to us all.

I might not be the quiet timid little thing I once was, but I still hold the core values I always have and will. To be kind and fair to each other, none of us asked to be born. We just have to help make it bearable for each other, and that is easier said than done. Life lessons have taught me that people such as me who were born with a silver spoon in their mouths should do more to help those who are less fortunate.

I'm no longer the wealthy woman who sits home bitching about the things wrong with the world without lifting a finger to help. I'm using the means I have available to me, (IE My sickeningly large inheritance from my Dad and Grandad) to make life better for those who are not as lucky as I was. I don't want to say what it is because I can't stand self-publicity. Before you say I just advertised it my surname Aricot is made up to cover my real identity

I think I've said enough about this subject for now. Time to get back into the mindset of my younger self. I talk a lot about myself here because Jessie is in charge and she wanted me to talk in my words about my progression as a person coming back from the accident that brought me to the brink of death. How surprisingly for me, my life took an upward turn on a night when innocent people lost their lives.

I have a great way to describe how my life had been at times before I met Jessie and Mandy.

You know those things on Facebook that tell you what movie character you're most like. The ones that tell you, that you are like a person who is much more famous and better looking than you. It would seem that they do these things either to make people feel better about themselves, or laugh at how ridiculously wrong it is. What these are really there to do is make you like the page so that they can sell their page after it gets lots of likes. They also take your mind away from concentrating on real-world issues. Children are starving not just in Africa and the third world, but here in the UK. However, all of that is forgotten when Facebook tells an overweight old man he is Rambo.

However, just say for one moment that I did want to compare myself to a movie character. There are plenty of hot young actresses I'd love to be compared to. However, if I had to choose the character who was most like me, my choice may or may not surprise you.

My movie character is Lieutenant Dan Taylor from the movie Forrest Gump. If you haven't seen Forrest Gump, stop reading and go and watch the DVD or Sky Movies. No actually don't.

So you're thinking it's obvious now that my reason for choosing Lieutenant Dan is that he had his legs amputated just like me. He had his blown to pieces in Vietnam in an act of bravery. I, on the other hand, drove my car off a mountain road, killing not only my brother and sister who were in the car with me, but my parents and grandparents in the car in front of us. No evidence was found to suggest that I I had alcohol or drugs in my system. People who I apparently knew claimed I was a good driver and never put a foot wrong. This was why my Dad trusted me to drive his Aston Martin when I was barely Nineteen. So who knows why I crashed?

Back to Lieutenant Dan. I first remember seeing the movie when I was shut away in my flat where I hid myself away from midway through 1997 until just after New Year of 1998. I may have seen it before that, but I don't remember it. Despite knowing how to talk, read, write and do maths, I had no memory of my life before the crash and even now I only remember little things.

My comparisons to Lieutenant Dan are more to do with the outlook on life after losing our legs. There are parts in the character's life that mirror mine more than others. I don't drink whisky and smoke or have sex with random people. But I did do some of the crazy things he did. Like for example, the epic moment where he jumps out of the fishing boat and swims to the shore. I've recreated that moment a few times, only it was my father's yacht in Monaco I jumped off, not a fishing boat.

Even back home in the cold seas and rivers of England, I would swim miles off the coast of Cromer and Sheringham, not caring if I drowned and often wishing I would. Again, like Lieutenant Dan, when a storm came over I would sit out in the rain and shout back at the thunder, shouting at God asking him to take me.

In the end, I found solace in the realisation that as I hadn't died with my family, then there must be some reason for me to still be alive and that I should do what I could to earn forgiveness for killing my family. I came to realise that there are many examples in the world to suggest that God does not exist. However, if he does and he is all loving, he will not send a person to hell for a brief driving error and he may even have caused the deaths so that he had more angels.

So, like Lieutenant Dan my life went full circle and after years of wishing I was dead, I finally found my purpose in life. I was only halfway to finding it on the night the train crashed.

Who would have thought such a horrible accident would actually change my life again, bringing it back around to a place where I could finally be at peace with myself, and learn to let people love me like I loved them?

At first, I thought it was all a nightmare, the train exploding and the girl who could read my past. I didn't really believe that anyone had the ability to tell me things that I did not know about myself and to kid myself that the part of my dream was real was just wishful thinking. The second part of the dream however was my biggest fear. The thought of losing any of the people in my new life or any of them being hurt killed me.

I was now awake in my bed in the early hours of the morning with my head under the covers, too scared to face the world in case I was still dreaming and the monster that I just saw taking my friend was in my room. But then I have to question whether or not Amber was my friend. In the time I had known her, although not unfriendly, she had always been quite moody and quiet, and without meaning this in a nasty way, self-centred.

It must have been a dream because Amber was the last person I would have thought of as risking her life to save anyone's life but her own. Obviously, I felt very guilty for thinking that it was not a dream and that she had in fact saved my life. Not only that, she is far from selfish and has become one of my closest friends out of the remaining members of the group.

The fact that I was in bed however convinced me that it was all a horrible dream and that everyone was safe and alive in their beds. I would roll over and try to get a few more hours sleep, before getting up to go for my morning swim and then go to work. Actually, forget the swim, my throat felt like sandpaper and my nose was both blocked and running at the same time with my remaining limbs aching. I didn't want to miss work so it was probably better to take some paracetamol and sleep off the illness in the hope of feeling better for work, although I didn't want to make anyone else sick.

What was odd is that I seemed to have gone to bed wearing one of my false legs. I always take them both off for bed. In fact I rarely even put them on at home, so I must have been so tired and ill that I'd fallen asleep halfway through taking them off after work.

I must say that I lost both my legs above the knee. You might have seen recently a documentary about a girl who lost a leg above the knee after a roller coaster crash. However, losing both legs above the knee is much different. The prosthetics I had were very primitive compared to the robot legs nowadays. In those days my prosthetics did not bend and looked more like real legs. That's why when Sharon's group found my missing leg in Part One, they thought for a moment that it was a real leg.

Back then I found walking very hard and I only walked when at work, and when I did it was with crutches. The rest of the time, like at home, I used my wheelchair or I'd walk with my arms. This meant I had great upper-body strength.

I instinctively started wiping my nose with a hankie found in my pocket, and then after a deep breath, I gave it a bit of a blow. I hadn't engaged my brain enough to realise that I don't usually take a hankie to bed with me, or go to bed in my work clothes. I must have been too knackered to get undressed.

I know there have been questions over our focusing on our talking about our colds. It's not an obsession (See what I did there missing a space) It's just everyone being honest about their experiences of that evening and there is a reason for it as Jenny explained in part one. Yes, handkerchiefs were one of the things I liked to make for people as a token of friendship. I'm one of those people who has a need to be creative and express myself while showing my appreciation for my friends. That's it many people probably threw them away. It happened to be winter and people get colds and in groups like ours, everyone catches it in the end.

The reason so many of us have mentioned it is because it was different from anything I knew. Yes, I had a slight cold in the week leading up to that day. But if I remember right, this sudden bout of illness however could be pinpointed to the moment I stepped into the house of the old lady Mrs Fish where I met Jenny for the first time. Other than Jessie, who makes herself ill because she runs herself into the ground for the rest of us, many of the others who got sick also pin-pointed where they became sick within minutes.

But of course, at that time I thought it was all a dream, but was to quickly find out it wasn't.

Feeling thirsty I leaned out of bed, feeling in the dark for my bedside table where I always put a glass of water. In doing this I reached too far and I tumbled out of bed, covers and all, landing with a thump on the grassy floor.

That was when I knew I was still dreaming. Grass growing in my bedroom? As if I would ever let that happen were it possible? So when I opened my eyes in a daze to see what the hell was going on, there was a bright light above me and the sound of hissing and the smell of cooking gas. Before I could sit up and assess what damage I'd done to myself, a young woman in a nurse's uniform stood over me.

'Are you okay?' she asked.

'Where am I?' was my reply.

'You're in a first aid tent!'

'Why am I in a first aid tent?' I asked in surprise at how slurred my own voice sounded.

'We think you bumped your head,' she told me with an uneasy smile.

I relaxed as she shone a light in my eye, clearly checking my eyes for concussion.

'Hello I'm Katie, I'm a trainee nurse, can you tell me your name sweetheart?' she smiled softly.

'Mary… no wait… Georgina .. Georgia …No actually Georgie…'

'You don't sound convinced.' she said with a quizzical look.

'It's Georgie' I repeated.

'Well, I checked your wallet and your bank card says you're Mary Aricot, spelt like Aricot International Hotel.'

'I don't use that name!' I snapped rather rudely, sitting up and taking a look at my surroundings. I'm not going to use that name and I certainly was not going to tell her I was the owner of Aricot International.

We were in a small white tent with no groundsheet. The ball of light I could see and the smell of gas came from a lantern which hung from the tent frame and there were two small beds on either side with a big green first aid kit lying on the floor.

'Where is this tent?' I begged.

'We're on the marshes near somewhere called Halvegate.' she replied quietly, adding she only came up from Essex that morning and didn't really know the area. 'What happened?' I breathed.

'Well I am not sure' She smiled, 'There was an explosion from the direction of the railway and we went to investigate to see if we could help and we found you girls lying out cold in the middle of nowhere.' She nodded toward the other bed where a female hand was hanging out. She went on to explain that she and her mother were both nurses and that her mother had gone on towards the train while she came back to look after the other girl and me.

I was asking all sorts of questions, the first being, 'Why the hell are two nurses out in the middle of a field with a first aid tent?

'It's some pagan festival thing to celebrate the winter solstice and they roped me in to help.' she replied, adding that she was roped into it by her mum and that she thought it would be a laugh. 'Some drinks and some…' she mimicked taking a long drag on a cigarette.

Something came back to me as though it had been buried deep in my brain. The girl Jenny who could read my mind had said something about her mother being out at some big pagan event on the marsh, that she was too young to go to. What if this was that event, and if it was, that made her real? If she was real, so was the train crash and so was the monster that took Amber.

'Let's get you back on the bed.' Katie the nurse told me, reaching around me under the arms.

'I can do it myself.' I snapped pushing her away. I tried to pull myself up but realised that the bed was a bit higher than my one at home and that I couldn't quite do it.

Katie however ignored my snapping and kindly offered her help again. Once I was sitting on the bed, I put my hand on Katie's shoulder and gave her a heartfelt apology for having snapped at her twice in the last few minutes when she was only trying to help.

'We'll blame it on the concussion and call it friends.' she said offering her hand to shake. Looking at her properly, Katie was a kind-faced young woman. I'd say she was very young. Well, much younger than me at least, and I was only twenty-two. I did wonder how she could be old enough to be a nurse she looked like she should still have been at school.

Like me, she had dark hair and pale skin, but her hair was rather boyish, shorter and thicker than mine and she was sweating as though she had been working hard.

Her perspiration was possibly from the effort of carrying me to the tent. I wondered if I should warn her or if I even dared to tell her that I just saw a monster take my friend out of thin air, but then I thought maybe that was down to the throbbing bump on my head.

I thought I had to tell her what I thought I'd seen even if she thought I was crazy. She knelt there listening carefully, with her mouth open as I told her about the train blowing up, but when I got to the bit about the monster taking Amber, she stopped me and said, 'Okay, sweetheart, you really did bang your head hard.' A mischievous grin came across her face and she gave a little giggle.

'What's funny?' I demanded.

'Well I don't want to dismiss what you're saying,' she breathed nervously, 'Or laugh at this horrible situation, but I heard that my big sister Katherine is out here somewhere and she's a big hairy monster. Are you sure it wasn't her?'

'Unless your sister turns into the incredible Hulk, I don't think it was her.' I replied trying to force a smile, joking that I had heard stories of people changing under the full moon.

Her reply did make me smile briefly. 'It's a good theory, but for you to turn into a monster under a full moon you have to not be a monster to start with.'

I wasn't going to ask a girl I'd just met why she hated her sister so much.

Katie, who had been looking me over as we talked suddenly turned away and sneezed. As she reached into her pocket and took out a packet of tissues. A pack of cigarettes fell out of her pocket and scattered in the grass.

'Please do excuse both my cold and my nasty habit,' she told me with a wry smile as she bent down and picked up the cigarettes one by one.

'No need to apologise, it's not like you're smoking them in my face.' I smiled adding that I wouldn't worry about giving me her cold as I already had one.

There was a grunting noise from the bed on the other side of the tent then suddenly the woman sneezed heavily in her sleep.

'Looks like she's got it too.' Katie said, going to stand over the other girl, where she took her pulse.

'Why haven't they brought the others here, I asked, thinking of Becky with her broken leg and Jim with his burns, they needed help more than me. 'My mum and her friends will find them and either bring them here or find a way to get them to hospital.'

It dawned on me as she said it that I had not looked at the other girl who was in the bed next to me. What if it was Amber and she had already been found and was hurt badly?

'I don't know how we're going to do it, but you both need to be in hospital.' Katie was saying, telling me that I'd been out at least twenty minutes since they'd found me and the other girl was still out unconscious. 'Are either of you on medication for anything?' Katie was asking.

'Epilim for my epilepsy' I replied.

'And if you don't mind me asking, when did you…?' She looked sadly down at my legs.

'Car accident 1996.' I told her.

'You poor woman.' She sighed, 'And what about her is she on any medication?'

It was a bit of a weird question to ask somebody, seeing as I hadn't even seen who the person in the bed was. I craned my neck so that I could see who it was but to my surprise, I didn't even know the young woman in the bed. She hadn't been on the train unless I didn't see her.

'I haven't got a clue who she is.' I replied.

'That's quite worrying that you don't know her.' Katie replied. 'Take a look.' She said, passing me the girl's wallet saying that she'd taken it for identification. 'See' she smiled, 'There's a picture of the two of you in her wallet and you have matching necklaces.'

She was right! There was an old picture of me with that girl, I had my own copy in the drawer in the top of my bedside table. The necklace I wore fitted hers to make a heart shape. I read the name on her bank card and began to cry. This was all just another dream because she couldn't be here. The girl in the bed was the girl my head could not remember ever since my accident. That lady was Maggy Grace Aricot. My dead twin.

Chapter 3 JAMES

I didn't write in Volume One, because there was enough going on and anything I took part in was covered by Jessie and Charlie. That was until they had their private moment, that was time for me to vanish. I must say though that I did not mean literally.

I stood there frozen while Jessie was having her asthma attack, not sure if there was any way in which I could help. When it became clear that she was going to be Okay and that Charlie was going to kiss her, I took a step back to give them some space.

It was news to me that they were not already a couple as I was reasonably new to the company and just assumed that they were together. If I hadn't assumed that, I might have been cheeky enough to ask Jessie out myself, had she not been my boss.

So, you're dying to know where I disappeared to while Jessie and Charlie were having their private moment? Well, I just turned my back and walked away for a moment. I headed a few metres back towards the train and then I looked back at the light of Charlie's head torch Then all of a sudden to my left-hand side I clearly heard somebody sneeze. My heart leapt, what if it was one of our missing friends? I called their names, to no answer, but then I heard another sneeze come from my left.

'Hello!' I said into the darkness. Still no answer. I switched on my own torch and shone it on the area where the noise came from, but all I could see was the long grass.

It had come to my attention that the wind which had been battering us from all sides seemed to have suddenly died. There was another noise from my left which clearly came from the field below the tracks. If it was a member of our team lying there hurt, they might be unable to speak. I called back to Charlie and Jessie for help but they seemed unable to hear me. I looked back over my shoulder but I could not see the light anymore. I was torn between going back to look for them and going to help whoever was there in the field.

I decided that Jessie and Charlie would not go anywhere without me, so carefully, I climbed down the edge of the track into the darkness in search of the noise. I felt a cold shiver down my spine in fear of what I may find.

What if it was one of our missing friends injured? How would they have got there? If it was anyone else, then why would they be there out of the dark? Those thoughts were crossing my mind when I suddenly stumbled over something unseen in the dark and tumbled from the track into the wet field.

I struggled up, battered and bruised from the fall, still looking for whatever made the noise and whatever I had tripped on. Suddenly, I felt a gloved hand over my mouth and a rather deep voice whispered in my ear, 'Don't scream, I'm a friend'

It took me a moment to compose myself and catch my breath. 'Who are you and what on earth are you doing out here? I asked the man.

'It's top secret. I'm not supposed to say,' was his reply. Before I could react, there were more people around us. I couldn't see them in the dark although I could hear their breathing.

'Who are you, boy? 'One of them grunted in my direction.

'I am James, don't kill me.' I shrieked in a most girlie voice.

'I just said I'm a friend, why would I kill you?' I heard the deep voice of the guy who grabbed me say as he released me.

'Are you one of the wizards?' The other man asked in a gruff tone.

'Wizards?' I shrieked, 'What the hell? Our train crashed and my friends are just over…' I looked to the spot where Charlie and Jessie had been smooching each other's brains out, in bewilderment to see that they had vanished. My heart missed a beat. Surely they were still there and I just couldn't see them. However, the space where they had been was empty.

'I saw them as well,' the deep-voiced man said beside me.

'What should we do with him?' A third man asked.

'Take him back to his own kind and he'll forget he saw us.' Was the reply.

'No now he's seen us we can't let him go!' Said another man.

'Who are you people and why are you hanging around out here in the dark? and do you have a working phone.' I asked them.

There was a moment where nobody spoke but the silence was broken by the deep-voiced man who said. 'We saw the train crash. Let's just go and find your friends and help. I felt him grab my arm and pull me toward the tracks.

'But I have questions,' I told him. 'Who are you and what are you doing in this place?'

'It's better for you if you don't know.' He said bluntly.

As I made my way back up to the track he preferred to stay in the shadows with the others. I could hear them moving along as they watched me walk to the spot where I had last seen Jess and Charlie.

In Part One of our story, Jessie made it clear that she didn't move for a while and that she sat drinking coffee with Charlie before they found that I was gone. However, as you may have figured out by now, things did not happen that way for me. I had only been away a matter of three or maybe four minutes and they were nowhere to be seen.

'Have you found your friends?' The man with the deep voice called up to me.

'They've vanished!' I replied in horror. As you can imagine, we know now that they are safe, but I had no idea what had happened to Jessie or Charlie right at that moment. In that moment of panic, I shouted their names. 'Jessie... Charlie!' I called. There was no reply.

There was arguing coming from the strange men in the field to my side.

'Let's go and leave him here.' One of them said.

'No!' said another. 'We can't leave him here alone, what if the wizards catch him.'

Again, they were talking about wizards. Why would wizards be out there in the dark, even if such babyish bullshit did really exist?

'Stop this bullshit about wizards, right now.' I told them, adding that we were all grown men and shouldn't be talking about wizards as if they were real.

There was a rather heart-wrenching sob from one of the men.

'And men don't sob either!' I said rather heartlessly if I am honest. The man who had sobbed so loudly then began to cry loudly. Stunned at the impromptu outburst of tears I wasn't ready to defend myself when one of the men suddenly came out of the darkness and slapped me like a girl.

'What the fuck did you do that for?' I asked rubbing my face.

I spun and shone my torch in the face of the man who'd slapped me. He was quite small and he wore dark clothes, but what concerned me was that he wore a balaclava over his face with holes for only his eyes and mouth. He was joined quickly by the others, who made their way up onto the tracks. I could see them all in the light of my torch. They were all quite menacing looking and every one of them had their faces covered with hoods, scarves, or balaclavas.

'Look I don't want any trouble' I told them, 'I don't care what you're doing out here, I just want to find my friends.'

'Well, piss off and find them yourself.' one of them said quite aggressively.

'No' said the first man I found, in his deep voice, now shining his own light in my direction. 'We will not be leaving him out here in the dark without his friends.'

'But we can't let him find out about us.' One of the others replied.

'We don't have to tell him everything.' was his angry reply.

'What like why you guys are hanging around in a dark
field in the middle of the night wearing balaclavas?' I demanded.

The man put his fingers to his lips to tell me to be quiet. 'I want to help you, but these lot might take some convincing.'

'Alright,' I said, continuing in a small, terrified voice as they looked at me menacingly. 'I don't want to be left in the dark, but you do look rather scary with your faces covered.

'Trust me, the masks are for your safety as much as ours.' said another of the men.

Just as he said it, at least half of the men sneezed. There was an awkward moment when the people who sneezed all stood trying to wipe their noses without me seeing their faces.

However, the kind one who had stood up for me, accidentally dropped his balaclava and clearly, in panic, turning sharply to avoid me seeing his face. He bent down and folded his hand over his face, but that didn't stop the blond hair which fell down his back as one of the others grabbed his balaclava and thrust it in his hand.

The men all looked at each other, then back to me and I felt two of them push me from behind, 'I thought you didn't want to take me with you?' I squealed. I sounded rather pathetic, but you have to remember these were strange men who were hiding out in the dark and there were at least five of them and one of me.

'We can't let you go now you've seen one of us unmasked.' a voice said in my ear.

'Don't worry though, we're not violent.' another deep voice said in my other ear.

'Wasn't it you that just slapped me?' I replied.

'Sorry.' He grunted

'What did I do to deserve it though?' I asked quivering as they guided me forcefully down the embankment and into the field.

'You insulted us and made our friend cry.' he said, adding that they now realised that I had not intended to cause them any offence.

'But why did you slap me like a girl.' The group stopped dead, it seemed the person at the front had stopped walking.

'Should we tell him?' asked the voice of the man whom I had first met.

There followed a quite heated discussion in which I was not involved, which led to them taking a vote via a show of hands. The result of the vote seemed to be three to two in favour of telling me whatever this revelation was. In all honesty, however, I cared more about what the hell had happened to my friends, and why they had left me.

There was some arguing and pushing going on between the men, but after a moment it seemed to have calmed down when another of the group decided to agree to tell me whatever their secret was, leaving only the one who had cried like a baby refusing to cooperate.

'Look' I said, 'If he doesn't want to it's not all that important.'

The man sobbed again, and again I wondered exactly what I'd done.

Then, as if things couldn't get any stranger, the first man offered me his hand to shake.

'I'm James.' I told him.

'I'm Helen' he replied, shaking my hand in a tight grip. This was followed by a second handshake with a man who introduced himself as Alice. He was followed by Karen, and he was followed by Heather, and he was lastly, and rather reluctantly, followed by Chloe.

I clearly wasn't thinking straight under the circumstances as I wondered what five men called Helen, Alice,

Karen, Heather and Chloe were doing out there in the night.

'So, is this some sort of secret transvestite club thing?' I asked. No offense to anyone who is a transvestite, but I was at the time, a very naïve young man and didn't really know about such etiquette.

I was quite rightly met with frosty responses from them, apart from Chloe, who seems even more naïve than me, asking, 'What's a transvestite?'

'Don't worry about that now.' Helen told Chloe, then turning to me. 'Let's make this clear, James.' she said in a very deep manly voice. 'Whatever we look or sound like, we are all girls.'

'Oh,' I replied jumping to the wrong conclusion again and digging myself an even deeper hole to get out of, 'You're all girls born in the wrong bodies.'

'No.' said Karen or possibly Heather. 'We are all born female, we have horrible disfigurements that alter our voices and faces, and make it really hard for people to look at us.'

It went dead quiet, I didn't want to say anything hurtful. If not for it being such a weird situation, I would have had more time to feel sorry for these poor ladies and ask again what they were doing out there. However, it seemed now their secret was somewhat out, they were going to tell me at least something about who they were and what they were doing there.

They were walking at a rather fast pace out onto the open marshland, taking me further away from any sort of civilisation.

'So, what are you doing out here?' I asked again.

'Guard duty' Helen replied, or was it Alice? I wasn't sure.

When I asked what it was that they were guarding, Chloe whimpered and begged them not to tell me.

'Well, if we are going to help, he's going to have to see it at some point.' Karen was telling them, adding that she didn't like the thought of me seeing it herself.

'But what if he tells on us?' she cried.

'I am not going to tell on you for whatever you're doing.' I reassured her, adding that I just wanted to find my friends and get help.

'I didn't ask you your opinion.' Chloe snapped back.

(I would like to make it clear that I am only writing this with permission of the ladies who have decided that anyone who reads this will probably think I'm talking crap, so it won't matter if they are exposed)

'Sorry about Chloe, she's a worrier' Alice whispered quietly in my ear. She went on to explain that Chloe was usually a pleasant person, but she was young and inexperienced and that this was her first time doing whatever it was they were doing there.

I was outwardly trying to hold it together, but inwardly I was freaking out. Whoever these people were, they may well be lying to me. Could I really trust them? My parents taught me never to go with strangers. Although I don't think they ever envisaged a situation like this where going with the 'Ladies' into the night was my only option.

I was terrified for Jessie and Charlie too, neither of those two would have walked off and left me on my own. Something must have happened to them, and I was terrified that with the talk I was hearing about wizards, that somebody may have got them.

We walked fast and in a straight line and I was talking to the 'women' but I never really knew which ones were replying as they all had the same voice.

They explained to me that they were people of the night who had to remain unseen for the health of normal people. 'We usually live hidden away in small flats in the city away from the open air' one of them was telling me. They were the low of the low, working night shifts in low-paid jobs where nobody would see them.

Chloe proudly piped up that she did work during the day as a cleaner of the toilets at Portman Road football ground over fifty miles away in Ipswich.

'I thought you didn't work in places where people could see you.' I ask quite innocently.

'Easy, Ipswich Town don't have supporters.' she laughs adding that she was a Norwich City fan. When I smiled and told her I was a big Manchester United fan, she slapped my arm and said, 'Nobody likes a glory hunter.'

We'd been walking for 30 minutes or so when somebody at the front said, 'Sure, we're here.'

'Where?' I asked, looking around to see what they were talking about, when I realised my light was shining from a tall fence made out of a black tarpaulin about twelve feet high and it stretched as far as the light from my head torch could reach.

The women pushed open a gap in the fence and pushed me through it. From nowhere a light nearly as bright as the sun hit me. As my eyes adjusted I stood with my mouth open. Behind the fence miles from anywhere and bustling with people and light and noise, was the biggest campsite I had ever seen in my life, even bigger than Glastonbury's musical festival. At the entrance was a sign and that read, *'Freaks of England Christmas village. Open 20th of December 1999 until 2nd of January 2000. Celebrate the Millennium with your own kind'*

A voice whispered in my ear, 'Welcome to the madhouse'

Chapter 4 Rachel

Everything works in cycles. In the springtime, a rose starts as a bud on a bush. As spring turns to summer, the flowers bloom in all their glory to attract the bees to pollinate them. Then, in autumn, the rose is an old person, wrinkled, and tired, but still wanting its last hurrah. Then in winter, the flower is dead and gone, but when the new ones take, it will never be the same.

Imagine if that flower is picked in its prime, taken from its bush and given as a gift from a lover to another with the best of intentions. That rose will wither and die before its time.

I suppose life can easily be like rivers. We all start in different places, we take twists and turns, some are fast owing and crashing over rocks, while others bumble slowly through cities. Each molecule of every river will one day reach the sea to start the next journey.

If the movie Final Destination has taught us anything it's that death has a plan and without knowing it the river of life can be stopped by a dam and redirected to the sea. Either way, our journey is cut short.

Death has no discrimination, if it was only for the old, then everyone would die like my great-grandad. Born twelve years before the death of Queen Victoria, he fought in the First World War and came back alive. He lived many happy years with my great-grandmother, living life, drinking beer and smoking a pipe. He lived to see the 1990s when he finally passed away warm in his bed.

I was eighteen when he died aged 103, and I can tell you he was glad to be going now that he'd outlived his wife and friends, and even some of his children.

The people we lost that night were only starting out as buds on the rose bush. Dying as an old man in a warm hospital is one thing, but young men cut down in their prime are something different.

In part one of this tale, I was very much in the background, which is the right place, as I was not central to what happened in the beginning. So I'm the boring one, I suppose you could blame my upbringing. I was middle class, or at least more comfortable than some of the other people in the group. I say this with no disrespect to anybody's background. My background left me talking a bit like the queen, making me come across like a toffee-nosed posh totty. I am however deep down more common than most people.

I married my third boyfriend—my only serious one—straight after we finished university where I studied to become a history teacher. After university, I went straight into work as a history teacher for three years, but I felt it was incredibly stressful and decided to take a year away to assess whether or not it was the right career for me.

I was lucky really that I had the luxury of being able to choose whether to work or not because my husband had a very well-paid job. However, he worked in London a lot and it was two hours away on the train, and he was out of the house by 6 am most mornings. Usually, I'd drive him to and from the station.

That was why the job with J&M was perfect because I usually got back just in time to collect my husband from the station, and the fact that we were using the train ourselves that week made it even better.

Selling health insurance is not the easiest way to make a living, but for me, I was surprisingly not as terrible at it as I thought I would be, and rather enjoyed it. That's why my year away from teaching became two years. I'd say the day of the crash had been pretty average, but it had the feeling that it was like coming to the end of a marathon because most people had been working six-day weeks for

the last three months and were incredibly tired and looking forward to a holiday. However, I'll be the first to admit that I was one of the few people who didn't take up the option of an extra day to make up for not getting holiday pay, because I didn't get enough time to spend with my husband as it was.

So, to describe me physically, so you can visualise me in your head. I'd say I was and still am average. I'm neither tall nor short. I'm not fat, but neither am I skinny. I'm not ugly, but no oil painting either. I don't remember exactly what I was wearing, but I like light colours so I'll say it was probably a light-yellow dress and leggings. My hair was sort of a light brown and I usually plait it, which is ironic because my sir name is Plait.

We worked in pairs and a lot of people like to stick to the same work partner, but I was one of the ones who liked to swap. Usually my work partner was somebody who I knew would respect the fact that I was married and off-limits. So, that was basically anyone apart from Greg. Only kidding, he isn't the worst, he's just the one we all poke fun at. I believe I'd been working with Rob that day.

I can confirm what others said about people being ill as well. I don't have allergies and rarely catch colds. In fact, I think that carrying a hanky all the time really came from my teaching days. You don't want to get caught short with a bunch of rowdy high school kids. I did use one of the beautiful hankies that Georgie made me, just to dry my tears when a client tells me something sad or happy. (Georgie is a darling by the way)

The tears tended to happen often. In fact, I think it's probably because I'm a big softy, but I'm also very caring. I'd gone into work feeling fine, and then about halfway through the afternoon, I just burst out into a horrible cold in a matter of a few minutes.

It started when I knocked on the door of an angry woman. I know door-to-door salespeople can be annoying, but we don't like to harass people, and if you don't want us to visit you, as many people don't, then that's okay. However, this lady had flung open her front door and before I had even had the chance to smile, she looked me in the eye, her face red with anger and told me to go and fuck myself.

I respect people's right to say they don't want to buy things from people at the door, but I was shocked and hurt by an unprovoked verbal attack. I'm not a confrontational person, so I was rather proud of myself when I grabbed the door to stop her slamming it, and gave her a good dressing down. I think the main points I made back to her had something to do with the fact that she had sworn at me for no reason and that it was the school holidays and there were children playing in the street who heard the "F word' she had just yelled at me.

The woman must have been in her forties. She was short, fat and red-faced. It was not just her behaviour that concerned me, but there was an incredibly odd smell wafting from inside her house. The smell made me glad I was not invited in. It was sort of musty, but at the same time like rotting fish.

She yelled a few more words at me for daring to stand up to her. She shouted something about everyone hating salespeople and we were going to burn in hell for making people's lives a misery. I apologised for whatever bad experience she had had in the past that made her think that way, but she just stuck her finger up at me and slammed the door.

I can pin the instant that my cold started to the moment that I smelt whatever it was in the rude aggressive woman's house.

Other than that, it had been an ordinary day, I wasn't really aware of the situation that other people described on the train. If I remember right I'd been sitting with Carol who was asking my advice as a former teacher on whether her son should do a GCSE in history.

I'm not going to rehash again everything that happened when we got off the train so I'll continue from when we found John.

I will never ever get the sight or smell of poor John's burning body out of my mind. I still have the odd night where I wake my husband up screaming in my sleep. It smelt of barbeque or a hog roast only it was a person cooking.

Without wanting to say anything too graphic as it will be too hurtful to his family, I still want people to realise how horrible it was. John was not fat, but even tall and healthy, muscular people have body fat which burns. John was a frying sausage in a pan. The stench was horrific, it was in my nose, mouth and lungs. I have never been so ill in my life as I was there and then, and I've had deli belly.

I think the whole thing of walking past the dead train conductor seemed like it didn't happen even though his blood was on my shoes because it was all so quick. The train was burning and we had to get off. John however was one of our own. Kate was his wife-to-be; she was having his child. Telling her he was dead was a job none of us wanted, but our own grief was also terrible.

It was the first time in my life that I broke down on my knees and cried out loud. I didn't know John all that well, but I know how it would have made me feel if it was my husband lying there dead. I wasn't alone in my crying. I was only sobbing a matter of seconds when Chris grabbed hold of me and pulled me into him. Within seconds we were joined by Carol and Ben and the four of us just hugged each other and cried.

It could have only been a few minutes, or it could have been an hour or a lifetime before we all stood up and discussed what to do next. John was long dead and beyond help, but the others who were missing may not have met the same fate and may still be helped. It was the hardest decision I've ever made to suggest that we left going back to inform Kate and continued to look for Amber, Jack, and Georgie in case we could save them.

The other three people had pretty much the same idea so it was a unanimous decision to keep moving.

We set out in our line again, searching the debris, now calling one less name. I tried to stop crying as we searched but just couldn't, and in the absence of a clean hanky due to my cold, I sobbed into the sleeve of whatever top I was wearing. I just kept feeling the survivor's guilt.

My husband would be getting off the London train at Norwich. He would be worried as hell when our train didn't show up, but at least I'd be home at some point and going to bed with him every night for the rest of our long lives. At some point, we'd even be starting a family.

Kate would now be starting a life as a single parent, she would not only have to deal with losing the love of her life. She would have to put up with all the whispers and the stares and the untrue rumours that other parents make up about single mothers.

With all my thoughts running through my head, I almost didn't notice that we had passed the debris of the train without finding any further evidence of our friends. We were now walking towards the Acle straight. It was shut for works and that was why there was no light coming from it. It was very strange for the road to be shut for so long and all night for that matter. The road has no streetlights—which is very dangerous in my opinion—still I could not for the life of me see why on earth the workmen did not have lights.

We continued to walk, shouting out names, but something was starting to seem very wrong. I was sure we should have reached the road by now, but there was nothing. The road is about two hundred metres from the railway. I'm not an athlete but I'm quite sure that if I walk for half an hour in one direction I can cover more than two hundred metres. So where was the road?

Others in the group were having the same thoughts and soon we stopped and got together to discuss what to do.

I was more of the opinion that we must have turned left or right and be moving along in line with the railway and that was why we hadn't hit the road. Despite thinking and saying this, I knew I was wrong, but didn't think it was possible. We all agreed that roads don't just disappear into nothing, but then we were all sure we had not taken a wrong turn.

The first thing to try was to take a sharp turn to either left or right, in which case if we had been heading in the wrong direction, then turning would lead us either to the road or back to the railway. Either way, we could get our bearings back and continue our task of finding help for our friends.

We stopped for a moment and had a quick vote between us on which way we should turn. There was surprisingly no disagreement whatsoever and we voted unanimously to go left.

Something I'd become aware of as we walked was that the constant sneezing from both Carol and myself had calmed down as we walked away from the train. When we'd been moving a few moments, there was a clap of thunder and the rain began to fall, cold and hard into our faces. Despite this, there was silence as we trudged on and with the ground beneath our feet getting ever more treacherous and slippery, I was the first to fall.

I wasn't hurt badly, but I landed in a puddle, which was so cold it made the rain feel like a hot bath. It was like having a thousand knives stabbing me. I was so cold I thought I was going to die there and then, had Chris and Ben not been so quick to pull me up. They asked me if I needed to stop, but in dogged determination, I didn't want to stop. I'd heard that stopping is the worst thing you can do when you're cold and wet. With that in my head, I took about three seconds to wipe the mud out of my eyes and blow my nose before marching on.

The difference I noticed was that Ben had put an arm around me tightly and placed my arm around him. I didn't know that I was quite sure about him doing this. He was a single guy, a bit of a charmer with the ladies, I didn't think he would use a situation like this to come on to me, given that he knew I was happily married. I asked quite harshly what he'd put his arm around me for, and I felt quite awful for thinking badly of him when he replied that he was just trying to keep me warm and stop me from falling again.

'If my wife was in trouble in the dark and in danger of hyperthermia,' he breathed, 'I'd hope she had a friend to keep her warm.' I smiled when he suggested that he would prefer a gay man to keep his wife warm.

I certainly felt more relaxed now that Ben had confirmed that he was helping me and not coming on to me. Aching all over and shivering as we walked, I still found room in my heart to feel bad for the fact that I got him wrong. I'd known Ben more than a year and a half and had got no idea that his charm with girls was just for making money and that he was actually married.

In the same way that my husband would want a person to keep me warm in that situation, I realised that I would be pretty mad at my husband if he had not helped someone in a crisis.

'I'm sure you'd have done the same for me if it was me who fell.' Ben said quietly and quite earnestly. 'I wouldn't.' I told him bluntly.

'You wouldn't?' he asked.

'Nope' I repeated, shivering and adding, '...because I'm not as considerate a person as you are giving me credit for.' I continued to explain with my face going red that we all continue to learn new skills throughout our lives and that kind of consideration was an area of my personality I needed to work on.

'As if I'd expect someone else's wife to look after me.' he laughed.

'It's called equality.' I told him. 'Anyway,' I added teasing, 'I'm sure Chris would do a much better job of keeping you warm.'

He laughed quickly putting his hand over his bottom saying he was worried that Chris may have a different motive for hugging. Chris took it in good humour, giving Ben a gentle reminder that just because he was gay it didn't mean he wanted to do Ben up the bottom.

This little bit of teasing was nothing more than a harmless attempt to try and lighten the mood. It didn't stop me crying, but it took my attention away from the cold. I tried to busy myself worrying about whether my husband would be angry at me for ruining my clothes. It was a bit silly really, because he's never been angry at me for anything. I was trying to take my mind away from the moment when we had to tell Kate that John wasn't coming back.

I shouldn't really have been worrying about how to tell Kate because it wasn't like we even knew each other that well. I don't know why, but I just feel that sometimes when somebody has to be told bad news it just seems like it comes better from a female. Maybe that's just me being sexist though.

Freezing cold and shaking, and probably going out of my mind, it took me a few moments to realise that Ben was not the only person with his arm around me. With Ben on my right, I found Chris, now on my left, and put an arm around him, and I saw on his other side that Carol also had an arm around him. It was like four of us had come together in solidarity to look out for each other and protect each other from danger. I think it may well have been because we all knew we had been walking for several minutes since we turned left and we had hit neither road nor railway. We were the group who had the simple task of walking a few hundred meters to look for help, yet somehow, beyond my understanding, we had got lost.

From nowhere there was a bright light in the sky that made us all jump. We were all looking around in a panic when suddenly Carol screamed.

'What is it?' I asked.

She replied in a panicked voice, 'I felt somebody touch my arm.'

All our head torches were suddenly turned on and shining out as our group made a second collective gasp.

There was a girl standing there. We all stood back and looked at her. I think apart from the initial shock, the thoughts running through our heads were who was she? How on earth did she get out here in the field? And, what on earth was she doing here?

She strangely seemed to hear what we were thinking as she answered the question in my brain before I even opened my mouth to speak.

She spoke in a rather business-like voice as we listened. 'Hello, you're wondering who I am. My name is Jenifer, you're wondering what I'm doing here. I'm saving your lives. You're wondering how I got here. Don't ask.'

We just all stood there with our mouths open in shock, and my mouth dropped even more as a light appeared to come out of the tip of her finger and shoot o into the darkness. The trail made by this strange light looked like a laser beam spreading its light across into the dark muddy field.

'Follow the light back to the train...' she breathed, '...but don't show yourselves.'

'B-but how d-did you do that thing with the light?' Carol stuttered.

'Don't worry about it,' she responded, 'Go back to the train, but stay away from the light. You're lucky I found you. There are many things out here in the dark less friendly than I am and Charlie here will confirm it.'

'Charlie?' I asked. Then, to my surprise, a rather pale and ill-looking Charlie appeared beside the girl. I felt Chris's arm tense against mine. Charlie had been walking towards Yarmouth with Jessie and James. There was no possible plausible reason for him to be there with this girl.

'What the hell is going on and where's my sister?' Chris yelled stepping forward to grab Charlie who looked terrified that Chris was going to hit him. However, the girl raised her hand and pushed him back saying, 'Just follow the beam,' and with that she grabbed Charlie and they vanished into the gaping dark.

Chapter 5 Charlie

Since we all got together to write Part One, many of us have got the bug for this whole writing thing and we decided to get on with writing our parts, so we can concentrate on having a get together when we meet up instead of writing. I currently find myself in Northern Ireland, I am here on business, but due to trouble finding a hotel at short notice, I'm staying with an old friend and her family for the night. That friend, who kindly took me in at short notice, is our former colleague Sammy.

In 2019, I find Sammy, now like me in her mid-forties, a different person from the one I used to know. She knows we are writing our story and has given it her blessing, but respectfully declines to take part or even read our accounts for fear that it will start o her nightmares. I find her to be only a reflection of the lady who we worried so much about with her heavy drinking and chain smoking. Her house is a drinking- and smoking-free zone and she makes good money running her own hair salon. She also tells me she has taken up rowing as a hobby to help her relax now that she's a mum of three teenagers and she does very well competing as a veteran rower.

The very fact that Sammy has changed so much in nearly Twenty years has inspired me to write my piece now, rather than sleep, because it's all turning over in my mind. So, after a goodnight phone call to my wife and kids here it goes.

Kissing Jessie when I did was probably not the smartest idea, even if it seemed the right thing to do at the time. Jess meant everything to me. In Twenty-plus years of being close to somebody like her, when she lets her guard down and allows you to kiss her, you have to. She didn't let her guard down often so that was the only chance I might get, to tell her I'd loved her for Twenty years.

Her kiss was like nothing I'd ever got from any girl I kissed before. Her kiss had an ingredient that I never tasted before. It was not the taste of coffee or the Ventolin that we just pumped her lungs with to save her life, although they made an interesting flavour. The ingredient was something more than love and it was just her.

Of all the times to choose, when we were supposed to be helping our friends. Both of us felt like we had let them all down and both of us were in a state of panic when James disappeared. I'm not saying that I regretted one moment of kissing Jessie, but at the cost of losing James, it was certainly not good.

Because Jessie was really struggling to see, I was very unsure about leaving her, I didn't go very far at all up the track to look for James because he should not have gone far.

I only went away for two minutes while I called for James. I would have carried on calling but I stopped hearing Jessie calling for James so I thought she may have found him, so I turned back to go and meet them. When I returned I found no sign of James. Jessie was quite still. She had her back to me kneeling in the middle of the tracks looking down at the gravel and sleepers with her head covered by her coat.

Strange, I thought to myself, I could have sworn that

Jessie took her coat off and gave it to either Becky or Jim to keep them warm like I did. In fact, all of the group who were not missing did the same.

'Jessie' I called as I approached, but my voice echoed in the darkness unanswered. 'Jessie' I called again, and again no answer. Then there was a noise. It was like crying. I hurried to see what was the matter, but as I did so, a voice like a whisper on the wind told me to stop and she raised her hand.

The voice was familiar, but it did not sound like Jessie. There was the sound of more weeping and I ignored her request for me to stop. She turned and took a quick glance, shining her head torch in my face. It can't have been Jessie as her head torch was broken. 'Who are you?' I called. 'Charlie, stay away,' she called in a booming Irish accent.

'Sammy?' I asked.

'Charlie, stay da fuck away,' she repeated.

My mind was racing, Sammy had gone in the other direction with Mandy and Sadie. How on earth could it even be possible that she was here. Where was Jessie?

Where was James? What was going on?

'How did you get here?' I called, 'Have you seen Jessie or James?'

'No, I haven't seen them, just run away,' she shouted.

'Why do I need to run?' I asked, approaching her with caution as the wind whirled around us, screeching in my ears and burning with cold.

'I haven't seen them since we split,' she replied in a weepy voice.

'What happened to Sadie and Mandy?' I asked but she didn't reply to my question. What she said not only surprised me but made my blood

boil. 'I hope James is okay. He's a good sweet guy, the type I would like to settle down with, but why the hell should I care about Jessica? Surely you hate her as much as the rest of us?' It was news to me that she was hated, Jessie was the most loved person I knew other than possibly Georgie.

I remembered Jessie, when Mandy had threatened Sammy with the sack, saying that she had paid for her to go into rehab.

When I confronted Sammy with this, her reaction was to spit and retort, 'Feckin bitch, as if she would ever help anyone eh? You and I both know that malicious slave driver is ripping us all off to fund her lifestyle. How many times has she docked your pay for something you didn't do?'

'I work for Mandy's side of the company,' was my reply.

What she was saying about Jessie was not right. I never knew her to dock pay. In fact she was always slipping twenty pounds or more from her own pocket to people who were struggling.

'What are you on about Mandy's side of the company,' Sammy said bending her head down to her knees. I could see she was using her knees to shelter a lit cigarette from the wind. She took a deep inhale, puffed the smoke up into the air and blew rings of smoke then took a swig of whisky, before asking, 'When the feck did Jessica give Mandy a share in the business? Considering they can't stand each other, and Mandy only stayed when Jessica bought the company because Jessica threatened to contact any possible employers to make sure she never worked again if she left.'

'She didn't buy the company she and Mandy built it from scratch,' I corrected. As if I didn't believe my two friends had built the company when I watched them do it myself.

When I told her I didn't believe her she shrugged and whispered 'Suit yourself, but people like Jessica are both the reason I need rehab and the reason I can't afford it.'

I stood back, shocked, as Sammy puffed more smoke. Who was this girl? The Sammy I knew was a loud-mouthed drunk and she teased Jessie a lot, but she didn't hate her. She still hadn't explained how she came to be here.

'Hopefully, the monsters got her,' She said calmly.

'What monsters? what the hell?' I asked getting rather angry at her now.

'The ones from your deepest darkest nightmares out there in the dark' she said softly nodding towards the marsh on her right-hand side.

I took a step closer asking her what on earth she was talking about, I mean come on, monsters from my deepest darkest nightmares?

My concern for Jessie was getting stronger by the minute, but as I strode forward calling her name, Sammy stood and blocked my path. It was not the fact that she did this that startled me, but the way in which she did it. She seemed to almost oat to her feet as though she was weightless, spinning to face me. I stepped back, looking up and down.

Sammy wasn't my favourite person in the world and by the sound of her, she was obviously drunk, otherwise, she wouldn't have been going on about monsters. However, the hell she ended up miles from her group I had no idea. She needed help and I couldn't leave her there alone. I took Sammy by the arm to bring her with me as I looked for Jessie and James.

'You won't find them,' she shouted out loud.

'Rubbish,' I told her, 'Jessie was up this way, and if I didn't find James back there, Jessie will have him.'

She shouted out something about monsters again and told me I should be running in the other direction.

'Well, Sammy, tell me this,' I added, pulling her to face me. 'If there are monsters this way, why are you not running away?'

In the light of my head torch, I could see she was very pale and her eyes looked a little bloodshot. I did wonder if she had had more than just alcohol.

Rather than answer me she looked me up and down in a rather odd way and she seemed to be licking her lips in a rather seductive way as though she was coming on to me.

'Stop it,' I warned her, but she just kept looking at me in that seductive way until she leaned forward and whispered in my ear, 'There's no escape.'

'From what?' I asked bewildered, but she just continued with a crazy smile,

'I don't need to run from monsters anymore, now they've already got me.'

I went rather numb and uncomfortable as she invited herself to kiss my neck. What if Jessie came back and found us and got the wrong idea? I didn't want her, but I seemed rooted to the spot and somehow enchanted.

'Sammy get off me,' I was yelling at her, but when I got the strength to push her away she stood there laughing to herself incoherently.

When I asked her why she was laughing, she simply said, 'I told you to run away Charlie.'

'Look for the last time,' I told her angrily. 'There are no monsters and we have to find Jessie and James.'

Again, she just laughed, keeping her eyes on my neck as I tried to pull her along, saying, 'Let's run, pretend the monsters are behind us so that we can run this way and find Jessie.'

Sammy refused to come and stopped still, her eyes looked grey and dull as she spoke, not taking her eyes from my neck. 'I drink and smoke way too much to be fit enough to run away from monsters.'

'Well,' I told her angrily. 'I'm sure if you walk faster it will help your fitness.'

'You don't understand,' she grinned 'I don't need to run from the monsters because they've already got me.'

'Whatever, Sammy. Sammy...?'

She was opening her mouth wide to show me a huge set of fangs that seemed to have grown from nowhere. I shuddered in the sudden realisation that she wasn't bullshitting me, and all I could say was a cheesy line from Little Red Riding Hood. 'My, what big teeth you have!'

She just smiled and whispered, 'All the better to bite your neck and suck out your blood with.' The look on her face was a terrible smile as she leaned into my ear and whispered, 'I told you to run,' before throwing herself at me, lunging and snarling at my neck.

I tried to push her away. I'm far from weak, but Sammy was a really big strong girl and quite athletic for a heavy-drinking chain smoker. I didn't have anything to compare it to, having never wrestled Sammy before, but her strength was something else. I thought she might well break both my arms in her efforts to sink her teeth into my neck.

Suddenly from nowhere two arms appeared on either side of my neck and I saw in a flash of light from my torch that there were two hands with mine on Sammy's head. I thought to start with James must have found me, but then another thought crossed my mind, in that Sammy had appeared in the wrong place. These were not James's hands, nor were they Jessie's, but whoever it was they were immensely strong too, despite having small girlie hands. With the lactic acid pumping through my arms and sweat pouring over my breathless chest, the two of us managed to hold Sammy back.

'Who are you?' I called to the person who so conveniently rescued me at such a late minute.

'For now, you can call me Buffy the Vampire Slayer,' was the reply that came in the shape of a very young female voice.

'Well, it's really good to meet you, Buffy' I breathed over Sammy's snarling. 'It was great timing, but what the hell happened to Sammy, and what the hell were you doing out here in the dark?'

The answer I got would have been obvious to most people at the time, but not me. While whoever this Buy was, she seemed to be holding Sammy away with amazing ease, she replied, 'Don't you watch TV?'

'Not really,' I gasped. 'What? You've never seen Buffy the Vampire Slayer?' Apparently, it was a hit TV show among teenagers in the 1990s.

'Never seen it,' I told her.

'Do you even watch TV?' She asked.

'No, I have a job, friends, and a PlayStation,' I replied, wondering how we were managing to hold a calm conversation while trying to hold off Sammy who was still straining to get to the veins in my neck.

Her reply almost made me laugh, and I probably would have done if not for fearing for my life. She told me that her mum worked two jobs and spent most of her spare time worshipping Satan, but still found time to watch every episode of EastEnders, Coronation Street, Emmerdale Farm, Hollyoaks, Neighbours, Home and Away, and Casualty—in fact, all the soap operas on British TV, the kind my wife watches (Or used to when she had the time), but I don't pay attention to.

One very odd thing stood out from that sentence, and I had to question it. 'You're mum worships Satan?'

She ignored my question and shouted at me to let go of Sammy and save myself. However, once I had struggled free, the girl who had so calmly saved my life was left to fight this mad twisted version of Sammy on her own and it seemed she was starting to struggle.

'What can I do to help?' I yelled over the scrapping.

Sammy started to try to get around the girl to get to me, ignoring the fact that she had another neck to bite right in front of her.

I stood like a rabbit in headlights, unsure how to help. 'Don't just stand there find something to kill her with,' She yelled.

'What am I supposed to kill her with?' I replied adding that I had not even believed in the existence of vampires two minutes ago and had no clue how to kill one.

'You and me both,' Was her frantic reply.

'Well what would Buffy the Vampire Slayer do?' I asked in desperation.

'Put a stake in her heart!' She shouted.

My empty stomach was taking over my brain momentarily and I thought of a nice big plate of steak.

The girl, however, somehow read my mind and told me, 'Stop thinking about food and think about finding the other kind of stake.

I had no idea how she had read my mind, but without a moment to lose, I dashed around looking for something long, sharp and made of wood. After a few moments, I found myself running down the bank to search the fields. More by luck than anything, I seemed to trip over what seemed to be a broken fence post. I ran with my lungs

screaming, back to the place where the woman had been fighting off the vampire which used to be Sammy. However, the briefest look around told me that they were gone, just like Jessie and James.

Just as I was about to give up hope, I looked up at the stars in vain and there they were, still fighting, only now they were flying too. I honestly had not been drinking or taking drugs. The world for me had changed in those few short moments.

In less than ten minutes I had gone from being in fear for the lives of my friends to kissing the girl I loved for most of my life, then losing her. Then suddenly, I was in a world where vampires were real and my friend wanted to suck my blood, and there was a strange vampire woman/ girl just standing in a field waiting to save me, and now they were lying. I knew this must have been a dream from the moment Jessie kissed me.

The sight of the vampire and the slayer was going on above my head and there was nothing I could do to help, apart from trying my very best javelin-throwing skills in an effort to get the fence post up towards her. My throwing skills are not great by any means and the post did not make it as far as I had hoped.

In fact, it went a few feet and fell into the eld where I had to go back to collect it. I have no idea about vampires or people who can fly, but it was clear that the slayer was struggling as I tried for the second time to throw the stake and again missed.

The slayer glared down at me and shouted something about me throwing like a girl as I went to fetch the post once more. As I stood, I heard a shout from above as the strange blonde flying woman threw Sammy at the ground. I froze as she fell at my feet with a sickening crack. I stood still, then watched as she stood up and straightened her broken neck and fixed her leg, bits of which were hanging out and spurting blood everywhere. I stood deathly still as she staggered towards me, unsure what to do, while the slayer girl landed beside us shouting, 'What the fuck are you doing? Kill her!'

Coming to my senses just in time, as vampire Sammy lunged at me, I held out the broken fence post and just as her fangs were about to stick in my neck, I rammed the stake into her left side, aiming for her heart.

All the anger was gone from her face. The fangs were gone and there was a look of terror on her pale face as she looked down at the stake poking out of her chest.

She muttered shakily the words,' I'm so s-s-sorry I tried to b-bite y-you.'

'You're forgiven,' I said shakily with my heart pulsing so hard I thought it would stop.

She pleaded to the slayer and myself, 'P-please, please kill me.'

She stumbled forward falling on the slayer. The slayer girl who only seconds earlier had been fighting Sammy, took her in her arms and whispered something in her ear to which she nodded. Then, looking her in the eye, the slayer girl pulled the stake out of her causing her to bleed. Blood was pouring out of her like she was a tap, and with superhuman strength. The slayer took a run up and threw Sammy full length over her head and launched her up into the sky.

As dying Sammy rose so far that I could no longer see her, the scary girl stood beside me, gazing up at the stars, and she said quietly, 'That's how to throw something.'

'Who in the hell are you and what did you do that for?' I gasped. We looked at each other and I wondered for a second if I was looking at our friend Amber and if she had been hiding these powers from us. Using the theory that there were two versions of Sammy running around and one was a vampire, then surely there could be two Ambers, with one of them being a witch. That's of course if you believe this was real and I hadn't just fallen asleep on Jess and started dreaming.

'I let her live long enough to warn the others,' She said bluntly, holding out her hand for me to shake, saying that we had not been properly introduced. 'Jenifer, 'Buffy the Vampire Slayer' Fish.'

'Charlie Cole, and thank you,' I mumbled, shaking her hand in disbelief about everything that had gone on in those few moments.

Jenifer then knelt beside me and told me to jump on her back. When I asked what the hell she wanted me to do that for, she just smiled cheekily, and said, 'We're going for a little flight to go and get your girlfriend, but first we have to go and tell your friends who are looking for the road that they're looking in the wrong universe.'

I wanted to ask what the hell she was talking about, I had just gotten used to the fact that people could fly and that there were vampires. A man can only think of two scary unnatural things at once. I wasn't ready to get on the back of this strange flying woman.

'I'll explain everything on the way, just get on my back.'

'Are you sure you can lift me?' I asked stupidly, thinking I'd rather not fly on the back of a stranger, but it was better than taking my chances alone.

Her reply was that she had just thrown a vampire about four miles, and so she was quite sure that she could lift a skinny bloke.

So that was that. She didn't wait for me to argue, she just picked me up with the strength of Twenty men and slung me onto her back, then shot off into the sky with me screaming like a girl.

So, this is the reason I ended up in the field with a blonde girl and it also explains how Mandy's group found Sammy dying on the tracks miles away in volume one.

Chapter 6 Mandy

Sammy and I were running as fast as we could. If we had gone to look for Sadie, whatever it was that took her out of thin air would have killed us too. We could see the village of Acle now, or at least we thought we could. There was some crazy shit going on. Sadie more probably than not was already as dead as that girl we found on the tracks. We had to get the police, the fire brigade, ambulance and get the army out here to catch whatever it was that just killed Sadie.

There had been lots of talk at the time on the local news about pumas in Norfolk. These were big cats that many people used to keep as pets until it was outlawed in the seventies, and people just let them go into the wild. There have been sightings of them all over Norfolk, and they were on the increase now that more people had cameras and video recorders. However, nowadays when people have smartphones with cameras on them twenty-four hours, seven days a week, there are no more sightings and the creatures seem to have died out.

Basically, we were of the opinion that the thing that killed Sadie had to be one of these beasts. It must have been out hunting the cattle in the fields and come across us. That however did not explain the dead girl on the tracks that Sammy said was her, or the fact that she had warned us about monsters and the devil.

Either way, whatever was going on, I can tell you that I did not fancy being eaten alive. We may have thought we had gone a long way, but in my mind, I worried that we had not even gone as far as the bend in the track. That would mean we still had miles to go and that didn't bear thinking about.

Sammy was not dragging her heels anymore, the fear of it all seemed to have brought her out of her drunken stupor. The way she was running you'd think she was an athlete, not an alcoholic chain-smoker. With her long legs, up against my fat stubby ones, she had taken a lead over me by a few metres and I didn't have the breath to shout at her to slow up a bit.

Suddenly, I heard her shriek out in front of me and I stopped to catch the sight of Sammy falling forward onto the track. As I approached to see if she was hurt, I felt my heart leap out of my chest. Then, as the track began to curve, it just disappeared. I don't really know how to describe it other than to say that the track just ceased to be. It was as though a giant knife had sliced right across the curve.

This was just not possible, railways don't just have pieces sliced off of them, not when they've been there for over a hundred years. I stood looking out over the land in shock. The fields that I could see in my torchlight showed no evidence that a railway had ever been there, let alone a railway that our train had passed over that morning.

It was just a field, but when I turned back and looked in a straight line where the track had been cut, I saw to my horror that the shape of the landscape beyond was just the same. Along the line where the track had been cut there were trees and hedges that had been sliced in half, leaving just half a tree standing there as if somehow the other half was still standing, yet invisible. It was like something out of one of the horror movies that Becky and I sometimes lie in bed watching.

'Becky,' I thought aloud. 'How on earth are we going to help her?'

'You could start by helping me up and finding out how da feck this shit happened,' comes a cry from below.

'Sammy, thank God you're okay,' I yelled,

'Don't thank him,' She shouted back. 'If he existed he wouldn't have made a dam cliff in the feckin train tracks and we wouldn't be in this mess.'

'Are you hurt?' I cried

'No, thank God,' was her reply.

'So much for God not existing then,' I retorted. 'I changed my mind when I realised I fell all that fecking way and didn't break me whiskey.'

'Luckier you didn't break your leg, aren't you?' I shouted down to her.

'You can't drink a leg silly,' she called up.

'With your blood-alcohol level, you probably can't tell the difference between your leg and a bottle of whiskey.'

'True,' she replied 'However, being a useless drunk fecker does take the edge off of seeing yourself die.'

Looking over the edge of where the track was cut away, I couldn't see any path that she could climb up, because it was smooth as a marble pillar. The embankment that the track was built on just stopped and became a field and then there was no sign of Sammy at all, even though I could hear her voice.

Searching the ground for her there was just nothing but marshes. Everything seemed to go very quiet and still as I searched for some sign of her while lying on my fat belly looking over the edge.

'Sammy, where are you?' I bellowed. There was no answer so I shouted again, but it was deathly still.

All of a sudden, I felt hands on my back and a shiver down my spine as my body tensed all over, expecting another monster to jump out of the darkness. However, after a few gasps for breath, I realised it was Sammy.

'You daft cow.' She was laughing, 'You thought I was gonna climb up that way when there's a bank to climb?'

The moon had become much clearer in the sky and the stars were shining bright enough for me to see Sammy's face with my torch. 'What the hell is going on here Sammy?' I shivered. 'I don't know what the fecking hell happened here...' was her reply. '...but I do think I know what happened to John, Jack, Georgie and Amber.'

'Are you serious?' I stammered. She nodded and reached in her pocket for a cigarette and offered me one. I was so desperate that it took all my willpower not to take the cigarette, but thankfully my willpower won over. I did however take a cheeky sip of Sammy's whiskey to calm my nerves.

'My theory...' she said through her lips as she lit her cigarette. '...is that this line is the end of the world.'

'That's your theory,' I quizzed. 'It's the end of the world?'

'Yep,' she replied.

I protested 'But, Sammy, the world is round. It's been proven for hundreds of years.'

'No,' she replied sharply.

'What do you mean, no?'

'The planet Earth, not the world,' She told me, as if it was a matter of fact.

'But surely the planet and the world are the same thing.'

'Not necessarily,' she said with a twisted smile. She continued to tell me that according to the law of movies, there could be many different worlds set in different plains of reality.

'So, Sammy...' I asked wearily '...Are you suggesting... that our world ends out here in the middle of Halvegate Marshes? Because I'm sure it didn't end here this morning.'

'Obviously not,' She scoffed. 'It didn't even end here when we got on the train.'

'Alright, so say I believe your crackpot drunken theory,' I told her getting frustrated. 'Why does the world end here now?'

'I don't know' she retorted, but nobody cut the railway down in the time the train took to reach us at the station from here. Trains don't run knowing that the track ends a few miles up the line. My theory is that the track ends here. There's a line at the end of the world which remains dead straight, but as the track is curved towards the line, that's why it ends here.'

'But that's nuts,' I told her.

'It's a lot more than nuts,' She replied 'It's a crazy crackpot theory, but it's all I've got.'

'So, what happened to the others then? Did they cross over onto the other side?'

'Maybe,' she said with a twisted smile. 'We stayed to the left of the track and the line goes down the middle, so perhaps they were right next to us and we couldn't see them. Watch!'

As I looked up, Sammy took a puff on her cigarette and a sip of her whiskey, then holding her arms up she jumped backwards over the middle of the track and vanished into thin air.

Mouth open, I walked up to the place where she had been stood. She was gone, there was just no sign of her at all. I shouted her name but there was nothing until suddenly she made my heart jump out of my chest. Sammy leaned forward across the line so that her head seemed to float in mid-air. I stood with one foot on either side of the line and moved my head from side to side. If I moved to the left I could see Sammy's headless body leaning over the line and to my right was her head floating.

After a moment, she turned and said with a smile, 'I think we both need another drink.

'I must have banged my head really hard when the train crashed,' I said taking the bottle from Sammy. She followed me and we sat down together on the bank close to where the track disappeared. My whole body was aching and the fact the track was gone was all the excuse I needed for a quick stop, even if I did feel a pang of guilt. Every second we rested was another second that our friends were waiting for the help we were trying to get them.

I heard Beckie's voice in my head saying, 'Get up, fatso, you've got another ten minutes walking left in those legs before it's time for a sit-down.' The thought of it made me smile. I wish I could tell her when I had the chance, how happy she made me. I didn't like to think about it, given the state she was in when I last saw her may mean that I would never get the chance.

Becky was much braver than me and more honest. She knew from a young age what she was and she let everyone know it. Me, however, I was older than her and should have been more grown up about things.

I don't know why I found it so hard to come out properly. I suppose it's just people's perception and I was scared that people would say that it was only because I was too fat and ugly to get a man. The comfort eating was in part down to the fact that I was lying to myself, and it was when I finally came out to myself the overeating stopped and my weight started to drop from obese to just fat. Becky had been a very big part of that. She encouraged healthy eating

and she was a huge part of my weight-loss journey.

It shouldn't have been hard, because when I came out to Jessie it took all my guts and I was worried she would want to disown me as her best friend and housemate, but her response was to say, 'Okay, I'm o to the shop are you coming?' I looked at her and asked if she heard me and she replied, 'I heard you the first time are you coming to the shop or what?'

If Jessie could react like that, then I shouldn't have been worried about what anyone else thought about it. It was people like Sammy and Kate who I worried about. Kate did not seem at all supportive of her sister, and Sammy had been loud and drunk and publicly bordering on homophobic at times. I was, however, starting to see that there was another side to Sammy though.

I took out my flask of coffee, filled the cup and passed it to Sammy as we lay looking up at the stars. 'Well, the sky is still up there, at least that's not fallen down.' Sammy said with a tired breath.

'Who are you? Chicken Licken?' I yawned. 'Na,' she laughed 'But, if we do make it out of here alive, people are just as unlikely to believe us if we told them we found the end of the world out here, as they would if we told them that the sky was falling down. Plus...' she continued, '...who exactly is out there that we can tell? The monster that just ate our friend. That would be just like Chicken Licken. Poor old Chicken Licken, Henny Penny and Goosie Lucy all go to warn Foxy Loxy about the sky falling and he just says dinner time and eats all of them, the ungrateful bastard.'

When I remarked that she seemed to remember a lot about the children's tale, Sammy stunned me again. 'I wasn't always a drunk you know,' she smiled 'I studied art at university in Belfast before I came here. I took an interest in the illustrations of Robert Lumley who illustrated ladybird books in the sixties.'

I remember reading the books as a child and I remember the pictures that brought the books to life being more terrifying than a horror movie.

'It's twisted,' she smiled.

'What is?' I asked awkwardly. 'I always thought those pictures in those books were painted by a psychopath who wanted to cause children of the world to wet the bed every night.'

She took another puff on her cigarette and tipped the whisky bottle back another time before continuing. 'Robert Lumley who painted those terrifying pictures was a good man, a devoted Christian, and a Sea Scout leader. He wasn't sick in the head like Van Gogh. He was a decent church-going man who wanted to use those fairy tales to warn us that the real world has monsters. Not like the ones he painted though. Real monsters don't hide under bridges. Many of them are terrorists like the IRA, while others are politicians lying to us in broad daylight.'

She took a long suck on her cigarette and carried on talking. 'Nobody listened to Van Gogh or the Brothers Grimm and nobody heeded the warnings. Chicken Licken should have learnt to stay with his own kind and let foxes come to their own conclusions about the sky. The three Billy Goats Gruff stood up to authority, tricked the ugly troll and got the green grass, but as a society, we don't do that. What if the troll was not the bad guy? Just some poor sod outcast by society and forced to live under a bridge. We don't listen to the tales and we don't stand up to them and we never will. We are sheep who follow the shepherds, we're guided by the lies on the news and we always will be. There will always be another powerful liar leading the way.

'But,' she breathed, '...what if the monsters do really exist? Does it really matter when we are dying anyway it's what we're born to do? Alcohol and cigarettes is the way to lead the race to an early grave while exercise and healthy eating just slows down the life that some of us don't want to be part of anyway.

'And another thing,' she added before I could get a word in, 'In a way we're as bad as the wolf in the Three Pigs, knocking on doors and picking on the vulnerable. Someday someone will fall foul of the fact that the health insurance we sell is a load of shite and all they're paying for is to keep the insurance companies afloat.'

'Well, is that a bad thing if it keeps us in work?' I asked her, finally getting a word in.

'Well, it keeps a roof over my head, food in my belly and gives me the means to abuse my lungs and liver until they give up and kill me dead.'

'You and Jessie are like the big bad wolves in disguise,' She said suddenly and rudely.

'What?' I demanded.

'Not in a nasty way,' she added, 'You depend on your staff to keep money flowing through the business. Each time I sell some poor soul health insurance the company gets forty pounds, but you pay me twenty pounds and keep the other twenty pounds for yourselves, because you're the bosses and if any of us were the bosses...We'd do the same.'

'You have a point,' I added feeling a little bad when she puts it like that. 'Why do you keep working with us if we're that bad?'

'Because you're not that bad really. In fact there are much worse places to earn a living and much worse people to work for. I don't see anyone else who works for a company that looks after their staff as well as you guys do. You're always buying us food and drink, paying our train and bus fares, paying for my rehab when my problems are my own fault.'

'Are you serious about rehab Sammy?' I asked her honestly.

She looked at me with a deep stare and said, 'Yes Jessie is coming to the first meeting with and I'll probably be going in after Christmas if the world lasts that long.'

'True,' I nodded.

She put out her cigarette and stood up, saying, 'My gravestone will say one of two things on it. 'Samantha McFadden died aged 27, in death just as in life, not a fuck was given by anyone.' Or it's going to say, 'Died aged 120, died as she lived, a boring old fart.'

'You, boring?' I laughed.

'Where exactly are you going?' I asked, following Sammy as she stepped down into the field. She grabbed me and pointed at something in the dark. 'If my maths is correct and this line goes down the railway, then the track turns right at the other end, not left and Jessie should make it to Yarmouth soon.'

'And if you're wrong?' I asked.

'Well I'm no more an expert on the end of the world than you are, but I can see a country lane. All roads lead to somewhere and it's best to save our friends if they're alive.'

'You're a star, Sammy.' I grinned seeing now that she was pointing at a tiny lane which must have led to one of the small villages on the other side of the marsh.

'Okay,' she boomed 'It looks like Chicken Licken and Henny Penny will be going to tell everyone the sky is falling after all.'

'Wouldn't it be better to tell them there was a train crash and the world is broken?'

Sammy laughed and told me that we probably shouldn't mention the world being broken we should let them figure out that bit. 'Hopefully, if we are fit enough to jog there, we can save your girlfriend and as many of the others as we can.'

I stopped with my mouth open, and gasped, 'Who the hell told you about me and Becky? That was a secret.'

Sammy shrugged her shoulders. 'You did just now, but everyone guessed anyway. No skin off my nose as long
as you're happy and keep your hands off me or I'll tell her.'

'You're not who we think you are, are you?' I smiled at her. 'She smiled back. 'Just when you think you know me is right when you realise you never will.'

It wasn't possible to run on the field, so instead we walked along arm in arm, singing Don McClain's Starry Starry Night at the top of our voices.

Chapter 7 Sadie

Hello, so my name is Mercedes. Like the car but everyone calls me Sadie. After reading the first part you may have thought that I was dead.

Then you saw my name written here and thought differently. However, you don't know for sure that I'm not a poltergeist or perhaps I am talking through Jenny from beyond the grave and she is writing.

Before I start, I would like to say that I don't read fantasy books or watch films. Stories about things that don't exist don't interest me. I'm sure Harry Potter, Twilight, and the Narnia books are great for some people, but I prefer a good detective novel or an autobiography, or an action film. Another thing people don't realise me about is that in my early Twenties, I loved playing PlayStafftion, and I still do in my forties but not so often. (Yes guys a girl who likes gaming)

So, here is a little piece about me.

Jessie has already said that I was from the outskirts of Madrid. That's not quite true, but I tell people that's where I am from because it's somewhere they will have heard of. However, if I'm honest, although I was born in Madrid, I spent most of my early life living in Santa Fe. Yes, you read it right, Santa Fe near Granada in Spain, not Santa Fe in America.

So many English people ask me the question, why? Why would I want to move from a hot country where the sun is always shining, to England where it's always raining? Well, I laugh and tell people I am just here to take a long shower.

Basically, the answer is this. While many English people move to my country to live out their retirement in the hot sunshine, I was more than willing to do the opposite. I don't like the heat. On a chilly day in England, you put on a pair of trousers and a jumper, but in the heat of Spain you can't take enough clothes off to deal with overheating. I prefer trudging about in the damp and the dark with a bit of a head cold to working outside at thirty-five-plus degrees.

I met Sammy back in Spain when she was on holiday, and I was working in a bar where she was drinking. Although she's Irish she told me she was living in England. When I expressed a wish to visit England, her reply was to say in her booming Northern Irish accent, 'You have to come and stay with me in Norwich. It'll be a laugh.'

So, I met a young man, who was working out in Spain. I was young and impressionable and when his contract was up, I followed him back to the UK. I burned all bridges with my family 'who told me I was stupid.'

It turned out I *was* stupid, because he cheated on me and used me as a punch bag. Thankfully I'm no pushover, and for the beatings I got that man ended up in prison.

With nowhere else to go, I turned to the one person I knew in the UK for help. So that's how I ended up living in Norwich with Sammy and she became my best friend.

Although she was my best friend, I only lived with her for a little over a year while I was healing. Sammy dragged me on a night out to see this band and they were awful. Sammy was drunk and off snogging this bloke and left me with the friend of the boy she was snogging. I may have been pissed-off, but luckily her kissing partner's friend hated the band as much as I did so we went for a walk.

That boy turned out to be the love of my life Carl, and
I moved in with him not long before Sammy and I joined J&M.

He did well to put up with me. I'm a happy-go-lucky girl, I do the things I enjoy in moderation. For example, I like to go jogging daily to keep in shape, but I am not an athlete. I also enjoy alcoholic drinks, but I rarely get drunk. Occasionally I even had one of Sammy's cigarettes when we were on a break if she offered me one, but I don't actively go out of my way to smoke.

Relationship-wise, Carl and I were solid. Chilled out is the way I suppose I should put it. He was a trainee chef and worked afternoons and evenings, so my working late suited us well. We loved our lazy mornings together, snuggled up in bed in our flat. Well, me snuggled up in bed while he made breakfast, because he was the best boyfriend in the world, and I was a lazy cow bag.

So, my friendship with Sammy was complicated. She was the big loud one who helped me to come out of myself when I was quite shy, and I was the one to calm her down when she was being over the top. I was aware of her drinking problem, and it was me that had voiced my concerns about her to Jessie. Sammy could be hard to handle, as well as being incredibly embarrassing at times. But, whatever she did, and however drunk and deluded, she was my best friend.

Okay, so having said that I don't drink much, I did have a couple of vodka and cokes in the pub around teatime. Sammy and Jimmy wanted to go in there and I went in to make sure they didn't stay too long, but Sammy was stressing me out a bit. If I hadn't of had a drink in the pub earlier, I may have been a bit more annoyed when I realised Sammy had put whiskey in my coffee.

What happened to the train has been picked over enough, so I am going to start by telling you what happened to me when I disappeared as told by Mandy earlier in our story.

I was cold having given my jacket to Jim, but I was warming up quickly due to the fast walking. I was suffering from the same cold that everyone seemed to have come down with over the past few days. I was fumbling in my pocket for a tissue as we walked when Sammy tripped over the body of a dying girl.

Tears were running down my face, and questions regarding how she came to be dying there were going through my brain. As Sammy bent over her and replied to the mumblings, I thought for a second that she was in a drunken stupor. However, I soon realised that it was something I didn't often see in Sammy, she was being compassionate towards somebody other than herself, she was giving that girl a friend's hand to hold so that she didn't die alone.

My feelings on the situation changed, as Sammy tried to tell us that the girl was her. Of course, I didn't believe it. How could there be two of her? However, I could not explain how the girl was carrying the same brand of whiskey and cigarettes as she was and in the same places. She was genuinely shocked when she revealed that the girl had told her people were raising the devil and killing witnesses.

I, however, had no time to question her about it, because all of a sudden there was a searing pain in my side as though I'd been stabbed or bitten. I'd been bitten by some sort of dog that had come at me from nowhere. I tried so hard to scream for help, but I had no breath in me.

I don't know how far the dog carried me. I was in such horrific pain, I couldn't even think about what the dog-like creature was or why it had me. I just wanted it to kill me so the pain would go away.

After what was probably only a minute it dropped me on the floor and began a snarling frenzy over me ripping my flesh from my bones. With my last breath, before it tore into my lungs, I managed a piercing scream for help.

I expected nothing in the form of help. Who would be out there who could help me?

Yet I became aware of shadows around me moving at breathtaking speed. I wasn't sure what sort of people could move that fast, or be strong enough to catch the beast. I only saw flashes of them in my head torch, but there were several faces. Within seconds, the dog was captured but it was too late. I was bleeding out of a huge hole in my chest and my small intestine was spilled out on the grass.

I didn't want to see my injuries so I closed my eyes in the hope that my death would come quickly. Just as I started to think things couldn't get any worse or any more surreal, I felt a sharp sucking on my neck and on my arms and legs. Terrified I used my last bit of strength to open my eyes.

In the light of my head torch, I saw the people who had saved me from the dog gathered around me on their knees. They weren't helping me, they were sucking my blood.

Everything went black, then the pain was gone. They say when you die your life flashes in front of you, then you go on to either heaven, hell, or purgatory. It was like I was in a movie theatre, watching myself on a screen.

Images flashed up of me with my mum and dad, and my little brother. There was a time at school, and with friends, then there was my move to England, all set to the music of Angels singing.

There was the time me and Sammy smoked weed just before I met my boyfriend. Then there were more tears in my eyes as I saw my boyfriend, Carl, for the first time. We were meant to get married and have children together, but instead I was going to be leaving him now. I couldn't imagine him finding another to take my place. I ran forward touching the movie and shouting in the hope that he could hear. 'Carl, I love you, I love you, I love you.'

The tears were now running down my face onto my top, the choir of angels got louder and the memories of my life on the big screen drew closer to that day, the day I died. All of a sudden, I felt an itch on my back, then a splitting in my back like something was coming out of my skin. I reached my hand around to feel what it was and found that a pair of golden wings had sprouted from my back.

But then the wings were gone as fast as they had come. The screen was showing something much different, in fact, I was now in the movie. There I was in the most beautiful wedding dress as my dad walked me up the aisle of a small country church. All my friends and family were there, even my grandparents. Carl was stood smiling at the altar as I wiped tears from my eyes. As we said our vows, I started to get a nagging feeling in me that I wanted to bite him. I wanted to rip out his throat so much that I couldn't stop myself. With a sudden pang of guilt as the vicar said, 'You may kiss the bride.' I heard the most awful snarl come from my own mouth as I sunk my fangs into his neck.

Suddenly I was awake. I was sucking and biting on something that was being held above me. There was blood pouring from it and I wanted more. Dark, rich, tasty blood was all I could think of. I needed it in me. Whatever had happened to me now was irrelevant. I was dying, but now I was more alive than ever and there was fresh blood all around. When I was alive these people were my friends. Now, however, Mandy and Sammy were not far away and all I wanted was their blood.

I should've been dead. Death would have been more kind, more final. This should not have happened; nothing could have prepared me for this. Ten minutes ago, I was worrying for the safety of my friends, and now I wanted to eat them. Unbelievable as it was even to me, in those few minutes I had gone from a placid friendly girl into a raging bloodthirsty vampire wolf. Thank God somebody managed to chain me up and put me in a cage.

Chapter 8 Jenny

If you've read this far into the book and you remember things I said at the end of Part One, I think any person with any sort of intelligence will realise that it was me and not Buffy the Vampire Slayer who saved Charlie from the vampire.

I must explain, if I didn't already in Part One, that like many of the other people writing in this book, I've changed my name to keep myself from being found. So, if any of you were worrying if your friend Jenny is really a mad dark witch, don't worry. My real name is something different, but for the sake of this story and any others, I am Jenny. I tell people openly in this book about my powers, because they will never find out who I really am. Even my husband doesn't know I'm a witch.

So, the first book ended with me explaining about my people and the fact that I abstain from using my magic to harm people, but I was barely able to use it for good things. My people had their killing powers stopped by a powerful spell centuries ago when the defenders of the earth surrendered their own lives to save the humans.

However, although I hid my powers from my family, I still heard their plans. There was a rumour going around that the spell that bound them from using their powers would end at such time that another defender of the humans was born and reached the age of eighteen. Seeing as the defenders died out in the sixteen hundreds that would not happen.

However, with my amazing ability to hear nearly everything, I heard rumours that a human family living in the North of England had been found to carry the genes of the defenders. Rumour had it that the two genes had been put together to create a baby. That baby would grow up in chains and be murdered the second she turned eighteen.

What was quite comical and rather embarrassing for my people is that the story went that the baby was stolen from them, and the redheaded witch, as they called her, was missing in action nearly Ten years after her birth.

However, that was just a rumour. What my people were doing that night was meeting in the light of the blood moon to try to raise Satan in some sort of bid to get their killing powers renewed. I didn't think for one second that they could do it, but I followed this group of people to make sure they got on the train home safely before anything kicked off.

As you know the train crashed and I went into the flames and pulled an old man out before being blown up myself, then somehow coming back to life.

To give you a better description of what I was seeing, it seemed that two alternate dimensions of the same world had crashed into each other or they opened out from each other. It was not symmetrical as though there was a mirror down the middle. It was like somebody had cut up two globes along the same line and stuck identical parts together but in different positions. There were two train crashes, one from each world, but only one railway. Each world seemed to be moving in opposite directions, so the two trains had been close to start with and could have hit each other but were now moving away from each other.

When I left you last, I was flying above the earth, looking down at the railway, seeing that whatever my people had done, had caused a major split in the fabric of the universe and two worlds had clashed leaving a line down the railway with different worlds on each side.

So, it turns out that the trouble for my people is that they were arrogant and stupid enough to think that they would be the only people using the open quietness of the marsh that night. They didn't account for the freaks' Christmas party, or the vampires and werewolves running around the place, and I don't think they meant to crack the universe. Or maybe they did because they're stupid.

So, when we finished the last book, I had just seen a mirror image of myself laughing at the chaos and destruction then she looked at me and flew right at me like she was going to try and rip me to shreds. Obviously, her ripping me apart depended on me not being strong enough to fight her. Although recently I'd been getting out at night and going to places unknown by my family, years of being locked away made me weak and unfit and surely even though I couldn't die I wouldn't win a fight.

I set myself to prepare my defence, but what she did caught me totally off guard. Just as I thought she was going to attack, she opened her arms and grabbed me in a tight hug and began to cry.

'Who? How? What the hell?' I asked, struggling to comprehend everything that had just happened.

She pulled away and laughed with tears in her eyes, and smiling, she breathed, 'Some proper shit just went down!'

'You're not kidding me,' I gasped pushing her away in disgust. Remember this was myself from the other world that I was pushing away, she had been laughing at the death and destruction that was going on below. She was evil, she probably helped to cause this.

'You did this?' I yelled, 'You think this is funny? You killed people you bitch.' Now it was me who was so angry I wanted to rip *her* apart. She had hugged me because she had assumed that being the same person we were partners in crime. I had heard that in other worlds, people were opposite of each other. So, by the laws of TV, if I'm a bad girl turned good, then the other me would be the good girl turned bad. Tv isn't always right.

'I didn't do this,' she said in a panicked voice, adding, 'I might have pretended I was in on it for my own safety, but please don't think I did this or wanted this.'

'You know what's going on then?' I asked in a less rough voice. She nodded.

'You and I are the same person, I think,' she smiled uneasily. 'I don't know anything about how things work in your world, but I always believed that there were more worlds out there. I was on my own, a lone voice of good in a world of darkness, death, and destruction, but I joined them only to find a way to stop them.'

'So basically,' I spat, 'You've just helped them break the fabric of reality causing the possible death of the whole of humanity like they wanted.'

'I didn't do it personally,' she breathed hard, 'I also didn't know there were going to be vampires, werewolves, and freaks here.'

'And these poor innocent people on the trains got caught up in it all,' I added.

She shook her head vigorously. 'It was all part of their plan,' she shouted as the wind howled, 'They need the people on the trains, the virgins and the pregnant women. They're not here by chance. This has been planned for months.'

'So, do you know what happens if they get what they want?'

'Yes, the end of the world as we know it,' she replied bluntly.

'Do you know how we stop it?'

'No,' she countered. 'You know they plan to do a spell which will raise the devil in the hope that he will be able to restore their power to kill humans without mind control. If they succeed the world will be over in a matter of days and it will belong to them.'

'So, we need to protect the people from the trains, and if it's possible, get them out of here. Then we need to

find a way to put the world back to how it should be?' 'Yeah, that sounds about right,' she nodded.

'Okay let's do it. Let's split up and keep them safe.' I said turning to fly over to where I had seen Jessie, Charlie, and James, heading along the track.

'Where are you going?' She yelled catching my arm. 'To look after them' I told her in frustration that she had stopped me.

'Of course, you are' she smiled 'See you soon other me.'

And with that we split up to patrol the skies and keep watch over the two sets of people from above, still unaware of the true dangers that lay ahead.

Chapter 9 Jessica

So, as you can imagine I was terrified. Charlie and James had disappeared leaving me nearly blind. Shivering and alone I had carried on shouting their names and thought I'd found them when I saw torches coming the other way. Somehow though, the torches had turned out to belong to Mandy and Sadie without Sammy. They couldn't possibly have been there as we had all been walking in opposite directions.

I could have believed that somehow, we had all mistakenly changed direction and bumped into each other. That however did not explain how Tom, the conductor, having died right in front of me had put his head back on his shoulders and come back to life. Neither does it explain why Mandy was giving a different account of what happened claiming that Kate and Becky were both dead.

I couldn't understand, it didn't make sense, not one bit of it. Charlie wouldn't leave me or James. Neither of them would wander off. Who were these people? This was not the Mandy I knew or Sadie. The crazy shit with Tom, I was happy to see him alive, but you just don't come back from an injury like cutting your head off. My heart was racing and there were too many questions going through my head to even begin answering them.

Then there was their attitude towards me. It frightened me more than anything. Mandy was insistent that we were not friends. When I asked Sadie what I'd done to deserve their hatred for me she replied angrily, 'Are you serious?

You're the same woman who last week docked my wages by £100 and kept it for herself so I can't buy my boyfriend a Christmas present.'

'I'd never do something so horrible,' I cried, as I tried to focus on their faces but with no success. There was a deadly silence as none of them spoke.

It was the somehow still alive Tom who broke the silence. 'Of all the people I've seen on the train, you are the most obnoxious bitch I've ever met.'

'How? Seriously how could you think that.' I asked, starting to feel tears in my eyes.

'Well...' Mandy said harshly. 'The way you behaved when the train crashed for example. How you ran up the train pushing people out of the way to save yourself.'

'I didn't,' I sobbed in a small voice, but Sadie continued the onslaught where Mandy left off.

'Seeing as you're here alone you must have left Jack and Sophie. although they might have ditched you and gone on without you, like I would have done.'

I tried to recall having done any of the things they were saying I'd done but just didn't understand.

'Let me get this straight again,' I sniffed, 'Remind me who went where.'

'Like we said...' Mandy told me impatiently. '...you,

Sophie and Jack went towards Yarmouth. Me, Sadie and Tom came this way. Carol, Greg, Mike and Sammy went to search the marshes. Chris, Ben, Rachel, and James went to the road. Becky, Kate, Ron and Andrea are all dead, leaving John, Rob, Sharon and Maggy missing.'

'But that's just it,' I yelled. 'The group I know does not contain anyone with the names, Sophie, Andrea, Ron, or Maggy. There's no mention of Amber, Sue, Jim, or Georgie.'

'That's because there are no such people, and you're a mad crazy selfish bitch,' Sadie shouted at me. The anger in her voice was like something I'd never heard from the Sadie I knew.

'This isn't right,' I cried, 'You're not the people I know, I did not push my way off the train first. I don't know the people you are talking about. All I know is that Charlie and James were here and now they're gone... And you,' I said to Tom, 'You were dead, your head came off right in front of me.

'As if! you crazy cow!' He sniggered.

'Look just shut the fuck up bitch,' Mandy yelled, adding that if I wanted to come with them I should keep my mouth shut, because none of them wanted to talk to me.

Whoever these people were, they clearly hated me, and I needed to earn their trust if I was going to have any chance of finding Charlie and James and helping my friends.

'Sadie,' I said turning to her with my wallet in my hand. 'I don't remember docking your wages. I don't do that sort of thing, but if I really did, then take everything in my wallet and I'll give you the rest when we get to a cash machine, and I'll even double it.'

Sadie was silent for a minute as though she was considering my offer and said quietly, 'Guys, I don't think this woman is Jessica.'

The others however were not listening, I could hear them moving in circles and sounding rather panicked.

'What's going on? I can't see?' I asked shakily. Remember everything was a blur without my glasses.

It was Tom who replied, and he sounded terrified. 'Jessie, do you hear that?'

I listened but heard only the sound of the wind.

'What is it?' I asked, 'It's like a rumbling noise,' Mandy replied. I listened again, but heard nothing until Mandy stood right beside me, and said, 'It's the sound of your massive ego crumbling to the ground while you beg us to help you,' and with that, she slapped me hard across the face and announced to the others, 'I've been wanting to do that for years.'

I stood there in shock, shivering. I didn't think I'd ever done anything in my life to deserve being slapped by anyone, let alone my best friend. But then she said we had never been friends. This just all seemed so unreal like I'd walked into a bad dream.

In the real world, every one of us is an individual who looks different from everyone else. Even identical twins like Kate and Becky look a little different. These people sounded like Mandy, Sadie, and Tom, but couldn't be because Tom was dead, Sadie was a quiet girl, and Mandy might be gobby and opinionated, but she would never hit people.

I did wonder if this was all some weird dream. It would have explained it all well, because train crashes are very rare in this day and age even in big cities, and rural tracks such as the Wherry line, which our train was on, just don't have crashes. That would be why I'd kissed Charlie because that couldn't have been real because he was still hung up on Jo and probably would be for a long while.

Yes, I told myself it's all a nightmare and that's why people are dying and coming back to life and that sort of thing. It was also why these people all hated me.

I prided myself in bending over backwards to help people, not for own ego. I was and always be just a working-class girl from a tough part of town trying to make a better life for my friends and colleagues. My worst nightmare would be to think that I had somehow done something selfish to hurt somebody.

Another theory is that it did happen. The train did crash, and I had been so weary after my asthma attack that I had fallen asleep on Charlie and *that's* why I dreamed of kissing him, but then the dream had taken a darker twist.

These theories however could not be proved unless I woke up. So, until such time as I woke up, I must be forced to treat things as though it was reality just in case it was.

Still practically blind without my glasses. I could only imagine the anger that must have been on Mandy's face when she slapped me. The surprise on my face must also have been a picture to see when Sadie, who had been slagging me off only moments earlier jumped to my defence.

'Mandy stop!' She yelled.

'Why should I? It's not like she doesn't do it to us!'

'Exactly' Sadie replied, 'You hit her, and she just took it. She didn't yell or hit you back she's just crying silently. There's some real crazy shit going on here and I don't believe this poor lady is Jessie or at least not the one we know.'

'Don't be a daft mare,' Mandy spat back at her. 'You're only saying that because she offered you money.'

'Again' Sadie argued, 'Would the Jessie we know ever offer back any of the wages she steals from us?'

'You have a point,' Mandy said 'But how or why would there be a different Jessie running around out here in the dark? I mean how does that happen? It's a mad idea.'

'As mad as the idea that Tom's head fell off and reattached itself?' I added, 'Or as mad as the idea that where I come from you're my best friend and that I left you walking for help in the opposite direction and yet I found you coming the other way.'

'You really think my head came off?' Tom asked inquisitively.

'I think there's blood on my top or maybe on my leggings.' I shivered.

He pointed his torch down at my legs and there was a gasp from the others of, 'Fucking hell she's covered in it.'

'Some of that blood,' I breathed, 'Is yours.'

He went silent.

For a moment or so I stood still having a coughing fit which climaxed in a rather heavy sneeze.

'That's another reason we're not leaving her,' Sadie told the others over the wind which had suddenly arisen.

'What, because she's sick like the rest of us?' Mandy said taking a big sniff.

Sadie took her hand off of me for a second as she coughed and she said to Mandy in a rather croaky voice, 'Jessica expects us to come into work if we're at death's door and doesn't give us sick pay. But do you remember when she broke a nail and took a day off to have it fixed, or when she sneezed and went home telling everyone it was the flu and took weeks off and was seen out clubbing.

'I hate clubbing,' I added.

'I remember it being the best two weeks of my life being free of her moaning and self-centred bitchiness.'

I thought I heard Tom laugh, but he quickly stopped, realising it was probably not right to laugh.

I could hear Sadie next to me blowing her nose slowly, and gently, almost as though she was stalling while she was thinking of a response. That's something I do myself when I'm put on the spot.

'My point...' She said when she was finished, '...is that even though I did enjoy two weeks of Jessica being 'ill' if Jessie was ill, she would be at home with her feet up eating chocolate and paying herself our wages... This lady...' she says grabbing me again. '...Is clearly sick, and by the look of her she's more ill than we are, yet she's here all alone. She might look like our Jessica, but who's to say she isn't another Jessica who was in the front of the train with her own workmates and hit her head and got confused...'

'There wasn't anyone in the front carriage,' Tom told her adding that he was sure it was me, but I may well have hit my head and got confused or was trying to pretend I wasn't on their train, so they'd help me.

'Look, whoever she is, it's obvious she can't see without her glasses, so we can't leave her here alone,' Sadie said taking my arm.

'Well, I don't want to take her,' Mandy scoffed 'But you can guide her if you want. Forgive me if I don't trust her at all.'

'You don't have to trust me...' I breathed, '...but please, don't leave me alone in the dark.'

'We won't do that,' Sadie told me, handing me back my wallet and adding, 'I'm not going to take your money, because although it's a kind offer, I'm convinced that you're not the one who stole from me.'

I tried to protest but she wouldn't have it.

Mandy started walking again and the others followed with Sadie guiding me, but we were going the wrong way. I tried to warn them that we were heading back to the middle of the marsh, but Mandy kept shouting that we were heading towards Acle, even though I told her again and again that we were closer to Great Yarmouth and should be there in minutes.

'What a load of bollocks,' She snapped, telling me that they had been walking for over an hour and should now be close to Acle.

'Look...' I said louder as I struggled to breathe again. 'Two of my team are missing out here, and I'm not leaving without them.'

Mandy ignored me for a moment and the second time I said it she exploded saying, 'I don't fucking care about your cock and bull story that you're not who we think you are, and you have another group of people out here. I think you're faking it to cover up the fact that you are a fucking clueless self-centred bitch, who has clearly gone the wrong way and has been deserted by Sophie and Jack because they hate you even more than we do. More's the fact four of my best friends died on that train because you were too eager

to push them out of the way to save yourself.'

'I didn't,' I pleaded, struggling for breath again, fearing that I was going into another asthma attack.

'Stop it, Mandy. She's really not well' Sadie snapped Then she whispered 'Don't worry yourself, if we are right, then we're nearly in Acle and we can get help. However, if you're right and we're wrong, then we are going back to where you lost your friends, and we'll find them probably looking for you.'

'Thank you,' I breathed, giving her a squeeze. As I squeezed her, I suddenly became aware of a big bump. 'Sadie, how far pregnant are you sweetheart?'

'I'm due in two weeks,' she said rubbing her belly. Not wanting to be rude, I enquired why she was still out knocking on doors when she was so far gone. I was sure that the answer she gave me was not going to be the answer that Kate had given me about not wanting to leave until the last possible minute because she loved working with her fiancé. Kate had John looking after her all the time, watching over her and keeping her safe. This version of Sadie was in a job wasn't happy in with a boss who treated her badly. She must be desperate for money.

I was right when she tensed and told me that the reason she had to work was to make up for her wages being docked by me, or whoever it really was.

I have to say that unfortunately in a commission-based industry, I can't pay maternity leave, no matter how much I want to and that's including for myself.

When I asked Sadie if she was looking forward to being a mum, she gave me a little squeeze and made a noise to show that she was unsure.

'It's going to be a bit more complicated for me than most first-time mums,' she told me with a sigh, adding, 'It's difficult because I can't expect my boyfriend to support me financially.'

'Why's that?' I asked her, adding that a baby is the responsibility of both parents and if her partner wasn't going to provide for her, then why did he get her pregnant? Her honest reply shook me a little.

'My partner is one of the loveliest people in the world. In fact, he's probably waiting at the station, worrying because we're not back. He's handsome and kind and we adore each other.' She paused and sniffed, 'He is many wonderful things, but the father of my child is not one of those things.'

'Oh,' I said gobsmacked that Sadie had it in her to cheat on her boyfriend, but almost relieved when she said, 'He knows he's not the father and I didn't cheat on him.'

For the next few minutes, I listened as Sadie told the story of how she left her long-term partner after finding out he was cheating on her. How she had found out four weeks after leaving him that she was having his baby and he didn't want to know... or pay. True to her word, as we walked she was looking out either side for any signs of Charlie and James while she continued the storytelling of how she had resigned herself to being a single mother when one evening out working she met Carl. The two of them had fallen deeply in love almost immediately despite her pregnancy.

In my world, I met Carl a few times. Despite being a model employee Sadie will be the first to admit she has a bit of a temper, but she was nice, and Carl was her safe space. The two of them had been living together for three years and really brought the best out of each other. They were one of the most solid couples I'd ever met.

I smiled as I told Sadie that Carl was also the boyfriend of the non-pregnant Sadie that I knew, and they were one of the happiest couples I knew.

She laughed nervously before confiding in me that she was scared that Carl may change his mind about her once the baby was born. She was terrified he would realise he was better off finding another girlfriend who was not having somebody else's baby. She had her heart set on giving him a special Christmas present to show him her love and how much he meant to her and how her hopes of doing so had been dashed by the other me.

So again, I'll tell you I thought it must have all been a dream. We'd been walking for ages and there was no sign at all of anything. Mandy and Tom were both getting rather tense at the realisation that I seemed to be correct in thinking that we were not heading to Acle and were in fact headed back toward the train. More worryingly, I wondered in my heart what on earth had happened to Charlie and James. Maybe they'd found each other and then gone looking for me and we'd missed them.

Suddenly Mandy shouted from the head of the group.

'There's a weird light up ahead. Let's go and see what it is.'

With that, the pace of the group increased to the point that poor Sadie had to shout at the others to slow down if they didn't want her to go into labour.

After a short time, we reached the place where the light was coming from. The group were gasping and swearing and panicking about whatever the source of light was and nobody was explaining to me what they'd found, obviously forgetting that I couldn't see.

Sadie led me down the side of the track towards the source of the light, gasping at whatever it was. I heard somebody come up to me on the opposite side from

Sadie, and then Mandy spoke in my ear, saying in a shaky voice, 'I don't know what the fuck is going on, or who you really are, but I'm sorry I didn't believe you or listen.'

'Why? What the hell is it I can't see?' I trembled.

'You were right,' Sadie said in a horse breathless voice, 'We're going the wrong way and you did come from a different train crash to us.' She breathed, 'The light is coming from the train you told us would be here.'

'We need to turn back,' I yelled. 'We need to go now!'

I had some crazy idea that I didn't want any of the people who were left at the train, like Kate and Becky, or Jimmy to see that I'd come back having lost two more members of the team and not found help. I didn't want to worry them with any of this weird shit that was going on. I wasn't even sure that I hadn't gone completely mad and made up these copies of our friends in my head. Maybe I was there alone.

A rather scary thought came across my mind as I gazed at the light. I had walked for more than an hour away from the train and at the same time walking back. That was without the time I was kissing Charlie. That meant that more than two hours had passed and there was no sign that anyone from our group had been able to raise help.

It also troubled me that with a train due back in Norwich an hour ago and another service due along the line, no help had been sent. What the hell were Anglian railways doing? Clearly, their train had not shown up and they would have known this when it didn't reach the passing place at Brundle. Surely they should have sent a rail engineer or another train or at least called the police, but there was nothing.

Mandy's group should have been in Acle thirty minutes to an hour ago and there should have been police and firemen and Ambulances but there was nothing. I would be hoping that the groups who searched the surrounding area for the missing people would have come back to the area where we left the injured and they'd all be having a drink as they waited to be rescued. The land, however, was blank and dark. Perhaps they'd all been saved, and our group was the only one still out there.

Then suddenly there was a moan and cry from our left-hand side. Sadie, Mandy and Tom all shone their torches and followed the sounds.

'Down here,' The voice sobbed.

'Becky?' I called.

'Jessie?' she called 'Jessie! They took Kate. They took my sister!'

'Who did what?' I called. All of a sudden the light hit her, and although I could not see what they saw I knew it was bad, because Sadie burst into tears, Mandy screamed, and Tom threw up.

Chapter 10 Becky

Hi guys and thank you for reading this book. After Part One, you'll know that I'm probably the most annoying person in the whole world. It may seem that I am an attention seeker who shoves my sexuality in people's faces. Just because I like bright colours and I run around like a looney, that's just me and I don't mean to be in your face as much as I am.

A lot of people nasty people used to call me a crazy dyke, but that's unfair to crazy dykes to compare them to me, because I was absolutely stark raving bonkers, until my A.D.H.D. was diagnosed way too late.

I have, however, mellowed with medication and age but I'm still me. I think I must explain that with this whole gay, straight, or bisexual thing, that I don't really know what I am, but I can tell you one thing. I love everybody regardless of who or what they are, male, female, gay, straight, young, old, single or married. I love everyone, and I hate arguing or fighting or conflict, and I make love not war.

I hope I am loved in the same way by all, but if I'm not, I can understand why.

So, what I had really been looking for was understanding from my sister. I'm pretty sure I was a huge embarrassment to her as she thought she was to me. I can't give myself any credit for helping her get over her drug problem. In fact, I'm sure I'm guilty of helping feed it while she was off the rails, because while everyone in our family was concerned about her drug-taking then, I could do little wrong.

I got praise for having the courage to be open about my sexuality. In fact, I feel that it was uncharacteristically selfish of me to rub my golden girl status in Kate's face.

Being twins in a poor family we had shared a bedroom until the age of eighteen, and I can understand if she was a little uncomfortable. I must add that being my sister I never thought of her as anything other than my best friend.

So, in reality, we'd both been quite awful sisters, and both felt bad and both wanted to apologise to each other but didn't quite know how. I do find it odd that with this being the case we still worked at the same company. I think in hindsight I'm sure that it was not so much coincidence and more the fact that we were keeping an eye on each other like most twins do, only in our case it was from afar.

Making up with my sister under these circumstances was far from ideal, but from the little chat we had, I think both of us were feeling a little silly that we ever stopped speaking to each other. I would much have preferred to be in a different environment where we had a cup of tea and shook hands over our differences and did a pinkie swear that we were not going to annoy each other ever again—or at least for another twenty minutes. That was what we used to do when we were girls. This was an entirely different situation, and we were stuck somewhere where neither of us could run away.

I was scared to move. My leg was so badly broken that I didn't want to look, the pain was so terrible. I tried to keep talking, to try and distract my mind from it. With the hand that was not holding my sister, I was massaging my nose with a hanky in an effort to try and stop the sneezing caused by my heavy cold. A sneeze would not only cause the pain to get worse, but any sudden movement could cause my leg and the bandages to move and I may bleed out and die.

I was overjoyed to see John wander into the light. Thank god, he was still alive. I'd been terrified that Kate would be giving birth to a baby with no father. However, he scared seven tonnes of shite out of me when he fainted. Luckily, he landed between Kate and me and he was still breathing. Sue had a very cool head in this situation, and she quickly managed with amazing strength to put John into the recovery position.

The light from the train burning was dying now, as though the fire had consumed much of what was combustible. Still, in the small bit of light that was left I could see the sweat running all over Kate and her contractions were not calming down. She'd been doing well to hide the fact that her labour had started earlier in the day. She must have been hiding it for hours. She hadn't said it, but I was quite sure that the puddle we were lying in was her waters, and that they had broken as she was running from the train. It was looking to me that if help did not arrive quickly she would be giving birth to my niece or nephew right here in this field.

On my other side, Jimmy had not said a word since he was laid there. As Kate caught her breath after another contraction, I gritted my teeth and looked over to Jimmy to see if I could do anything for him. I could make out his fast breathing from the pile of wet coats that were on top of him as they rose and fell. I tried to talk to him, knowing that the horrific pain would make it hard for him to reply. I thought even if he couldn't speak, me talking to him might well help save him if it meant my voice gave him something to keep him alert.

I knew that he had a deep affection for our friend Georgie, with whom he had worked on a daily basis for nearly two years. She was like a daughter to him, and I felt that keeping his hopes up that she would be found alive might do something to keep him going.

I was talking when Jim, who was looking up suddenly whispered, 'Andrea, is that you gossiping old girl?'

'Who's Andrea, Jim?' Kate asked in a hesitant voice.

'Andrea talking in my ear,' he grunted 'Getting closer. Come to take me home.'

Kate asked if Andrea had pointed out that taking him to a hospital was a better idea and asked how he had been in contact as there was no phone signal.

When she asked that we all went silent. 'Did I say something wrong?' She asked seeming totally unaware of the gaff she had just made. To be fair to my sister, she was a private girl who didn't mingle much with the rest of the staff and may not have had the occasion to speak in depth with Jimmy as I had done.

'Andrea is his wife,' Sue told her in a hushed voice.

'Oh, I'm sorry,' she said, sounding rather shocked, looking from Jim to Sue.

'What is it, K?' I grimaced.

She took a deep breath, looked uneasily at Sue, and said, 'Well I always thought Jimmy was your husband.'

Sue looked as though she might laugh if Kate hadn't got it so wrong. Sue, who had always seemed very straight-laced, said in a tight-lipped voice, 'My husband is seventy. He's at home with a can of beer watching porn.' She said it in such a straight-laced voice that both Kate and I had to hold ourselves to prevent us from laughing in case it caused Kate to contract, or my leg to move.

This was made worse when Jimmy suddenly muttered, 'Good old Harry's in the best place.'

'Jimmy was best man at Sue's wedding,' I told Kate quietly, although Jimmy must have heard me.

'I took the best woman home too, didn't I my gal?' He replied, still looking up at the stars.

'Why are you looking at the stars Jim?' Kate asked, looking concerned as she tried to get some response from John, who for whatever reason was still out cold. I was sure John had said something about having seen Kate die just before he fainted.

I looked from Jim to Kate and rubbed her shoulder, telling her quietly, 'Jimmy's wife, Andria, died from cancer forty-three years ago, and he never re-married or had children.'

'Sorry Jim,' Kate told him, just as another contraction hit her.

'She's coming for me,' he breathed. 'I heard her calling, but the girl got me off the train when it was my time to go.'

'What girl, Jim?' I asked trying to turn my head enough to look him in the eye.

'The blonde one on the train.'

'You mean Sharon, or Sammy?' I asked but he shook his head.

He said between breaths, 'Young Amber,' He sobbed, 'Misunderstood kind sweet thing should have left me to die and saved herself.'

'What happened to her?' Sue asked looking over to the train, as she too tried to bring John around by slapping him.

'Why didn't you say something?' Kate yelled at him. She said some words that were uncalled for as she shouted at him, saying people had gone looking for her when he knew she was still on the train and may well have needed help if she was still alive.

She took back her words, however, when I told her not to be too harsh on Jimmy as he was hard with it, seeing as he had burns all over his body and was in desperate pain, as were we all. I must admit that I hadn't seen her get off the train on account that I had been a little bothered by the fact that my leg was hanging off.

Kate herself also couldn't remember seeing her get off, but others in the group had been sure they had seen her get off the train with Jack and Georgie before all three disappeared.

Obviously, this was the case, because Amber is alive and has written in both Parts One and Two of our story. However, at the time we had no reason not to believe Jimmy's tearful confession that she had got back on to the train and saved him and that he had seen the fear in her eyes as the train had exploded, killing her with it.

He cried as he spoke again saying that he wished he'd died in her place. The most chilling thing he said was that he hadn't died on the train like he wished he had.

'You're not going to die with Sue here to look after us all,' I assured him. Sue however smiled and told me it had been many years since she was a nurse.

'During the war,' Jim roared suddenly turning from tears to laughter as though it was a private joke.

'I didn't think you were that old!' I said to Sue.

'Not the World War, the Korean War.' She smiled awkwardly.

'I thought you were at the battle of Waterloo' Jimmy coughed.

'I see you haven't grown up much in the nearly Fifty years I've known you,' Sue smiled. It was the kind of banter

you only see in old friends.

Kate was bending over, whispering, 'I love you,' to

John, and kissing his head. I was so happy for her that he was back and that he was not killed on the train, but at the same time I was sad for Amber.

'She should have left me,' Jim was sobbing, 'Poor young girl, with her life ahead of her, saving an old man who should be propping up tombstones.'

I was breathing fast, but the pain in my leg was now overtaken by a pain in my heart that was indescribable unless you have felt it yourself. It was not just the cramping pain you get from the shock of the loss of a friend, and yes, I did class Amber as a friend, even though she had her moments where we all wanted to kill her.

It was the awkward pain you get when an old person cries. When a child cries it's over something trivial which can be made better by giving them a cuddle and telling them they're loved, and usually sweets help. When an old person cries, especially a man when they are hurting deeply, a young person, like me, can only begin to understand why. Of course, he was as devastated at the loss of Amber as we all were, but it seemed there was something more to his tears and I was right.

'You can't think like that Jim,' I soothed. 'She saved you knowing the risks. She would want you to go on and live and not feel like this. She would have wanted you to live.'

His reply really wrenched at my heartstrings and made me wish I had never said what I said.

'You don't truly know how other people are feeling and how they see their own lives.' His question was, 'When you can't spend your life with the person you want, is it so worth living?'

'I don't have an answer to that,' I replied quite honestly.

Jim took a rattling breath the sound of which told me every bit of pain he was in. 'I had all that these two have ahead of them,' he wheezed. I assumed he was talking about Kate and John as he went on to talk about the fact they were deeply in love and starting a family. 'And then cancer took my Andrea from me before we could have a family.' He took another deep rattling breath. 'Nearly fifty years of wishing you weren't alive every day can take its toll on a man. A man who left it too long to look elsewhere for happiness.'

'I understand,' I told him, grimacing through my own unbearable pain, 'Believe me if I was 45 years older, or you were Forty years younger, I may well have been interested.'

His chest heaved again, and he almost laughed as he breathed, 'Thought you liked girls, young Becky?'

'Na, I love everyone, Jim, so there's hope for you yet,' I teased.

As I teased him, I put my hand out to find him, but he yelped in pain, so instead of holding his hand I just touched his skin. I hoped I had managed to keep his spirits up with our talk. It was all true, if it was not for the forty-nine-year age gap, I could have been content with a guy like Jimmy, despite my preference for ladies. Not wanting to believe that Amber had died on the train, we continued to speculate as to what might have happened to our other missing friends, Jack and Georgie.

'If Georgie is alive she wouldn't want you to die,' I told Jim.

'Poor kid made it on her own without her legs for years before she met me,' He huffed adding, 'Although she is the closest thing to a family I'll ever have. I love working with her, but she'll have to find a new work partner soon enough.'

'Don't be daft Jim,' I smiled uneasily. 'It's amazing what surgery they can do for burns these days. You'll be back at work in a few weeks and by the feel of this leg, you'll be back at work before me.'

His reply caught me cold. 'Don't matter what they do with burns. Not when stage four cancer in my lungs says I'll die a painful death in weeks.'

'Jim,' I breathed. 'Why didn't you—'

'My business,' he interrupted, 'I knew I was well-liked and didn't want to cause any upset.'

'But Jim,' Kate sobbed, turning to face him. 'If we'd known we would have—'

'Felt sorry for me like I don't want people to,' he said bluntly, 'Do me a favour girl,' he said, talking to Kate. 'I may not know you well, but we're all proud of you for coming off of the drugs. Make sure you stay off them and love that family of yours now you got your fella back.'

'I promise' She said tearfully, looking at Jim and holding John's hand, 'No drugs, and not a glass of alcohol, or a cigarette, will touch my lips again.'

'I didn't mean you had to be boring,' he wheezed 'The odd drink doesn't hurt, but smoking maybe not, because the pain of this cancer is killing me.' He turned to me, 'And you, be yourself and don't let anyone stop you.'

I nodded, 'Don't sound like you're saying goodbye Jim,' I told him.

Suddenly there was a noise from my left-hand side. On the other side of Kate, John was waking up and he was looking her over. 'I had the most horrible dream' He breathed sharply to Kate, 'There was a train crash, and you and the baby and Becky died and…' He paused and looked at me and said to Kate, 'Hang on, so you two didn't get on and now she's in our bed. What is this, some freaky twin-style threesome?'

'The train crashed, your girlfriend is in labour, your future sister-in-law has an open fracture, and you for some reason wandered off, then feinted.' Sue told him in a rather business-like way. 'And Jimmy's badly…'

I looked over towards him in the dying light and felt for his hand, but it was still. I couldn't see any sign that he was moving. 'Jimmy,' I screeched 'Jimmy, wake up,' but there was no movement.

Sue quickly moved over to Jimmy to check on him. She was slapping his face, but there was no response from him. I saw Kate burst into silent tears just as another contraction hit her and the hard squeeze on my hand drew my attention to her briefly. I don't think I wanted it to hit me that Jimmy may well have passed away right next to me. Jimmy's sudden passing may have been the most horrible thing ever to happen in my life, had it not been for the sudden twist of events that happened in the seconds that followed.

There was a sudden shout from behind us and before I had time to look around me to see what it was, there were people crowded around Kate, picking her up.

Thank god, I thought to myself, *they must be paramedics or first aiders coming to help.* But then paramedics wore uniforms, and these people were wearing rather scary masks. They picked up my sister who was screaming for help, and they put her on their shoulders. John was still very dazed from his fainting spell, but still, he tried to fight them off. Sue stood up from where she had been looking after Jimmy, who was still motionless. She ran over towards the people in masks, roaring at them to put Kate down.

As poor old Sue launched herself at the group of people to try to help my sister, somebody hit her from behind with a blunt object. Sue seemed to fall in slow motion, towards my already-fractured leg. The pain was like nothing I can ever describe when Sue's limp body came crashing down on my leg causing the fracture to re-open and blood to trickle from my body at a rate that meant I was going to bleed out and die. John had gone running after Kate and the masked people who took her. Sue lay motionless on me as I called her name.

All sorts of things were going through my head. *Who were they? Where did they come from? Why did they take my sister?* Kate's torch was lying on the floor and I picked it up, screaming for her and John as I grabbed Sue in my other hand to roll her over so that she could breathe. However,

all my hand felt was this odd gooey slimy stuff with lumps in it. I turned on the torch to see what it was that was running all over me.

Nearly Twenty years later, in my deepest darkest nightmares, I still see Sue's motionless body lying face down on me. The gooey liquid was blood leaking from a horrific wound on Sue's head, and the lumps within it were chunks of her brain.

Chapter 11 Georgie

As I sit here in the garden on a day in May, which they tell us is the hottest since the 1970's, I can still hear Jennie's words echo across time as though we were in the same room. That's probably because she's one of my best friends and she's in my pool, playing with the kids right now.

The words I'm talking about are the words she said as I was leaving her Grandmother's house. 'The spirits have a message for you. 'When worlds collide, you shall meet your Grace, and the key to your survival will be Amber.'

She had been right about the first thing when Amber saved me, so it was a sure thing that she would be right about the second at some point, but worlds colliding sounded horrible. Meeting my Grace made it sound like I was going to meet God.

As I sat there, looking over at the girl in the bed, I realised that my life would never be the same again. My Grace was nothing to do with a god I didn't even believe in. Grace was what my twin sister, Margret Grace, called herself. Just like I call myself Georgie, when my real name is Mary Georgia.

I would have known what my twin sister was called if I could remember her, but couldn't remember her for the very reason she could not be in that bed. Margret Grace Aricot died in Switzerland in 1996 in a car driven by me. There was no way this girl in the bed could be her, but in the same way there was no way she could not be her. She had pictures of us together in her wallet—the same ones that I put away in boxes.

The half a heart-shaped necklace that I had around my neck fitted hers.

How could someone who died in 1996 be alive in the middle of a field in 1999. Katie seemed to think that the two of us had both been on the train. That was not possible. I was still at a loss to get my head around why there was a first aid tent out in the field.

Katie had to explain to me several times about the fact she was covering first aid for her mother's coven of Wiccans who had come to celebrate the winter solstice.

Katie was only very young for a nurse, but I had to keep reminding myself that she had told me she was only a trainee. When I told her how grateful I was, she just smiled and said I was being too nice.

'I'm hardly the epitome of professionalism,' she laughed ironically, popping a cigarette in her mouth as she headed for the door.

I took off my remaining leg and sat there with just my stumps, holding the hand of the girl in the bed, while Katie was poking her head out of the tent to smoke. I was sure I could feel the girl, gripping my hand. I was willing her to wake up, so I could sort it all out in my head, and we could clear up why this girl seemed to be my dead sister.

There is always the chance that you will meet somebody in your life with the same name as somebody you know, or a family member. That's what it must be. She just had the same name as my sister and looked a bit like her.

Her sister in the picture just looked a lot like me and was wearing the same clothes. Her sister had legs and I didn't, but then the pictures I had were taken before I lost my legs.

The truth would come out when she woke up. As Katie finished her cigarette and came back towards us she was stopped in her tracks by a big sneeze. The noise of Katie's sneeze made the woman in the bed stir. As I held my breath she began to come round.

A warm mist came over me as her eyes opened and she gave me a big loving smile. She croaked 'I-I-I had a really horrible dream. I thought it was real. I dreamed you died in a car crash years ago and it was my fault.'

'Well, I'm not dead, that's for sure.' I breathed shakily. She seemed to have no idea how confused I was by the fact she was there and she was alive.

She rolled her eyes dopily and said, 'From the feel of my head that must have been one hell of a night out.' Then, she reached out her hand, telling me 'a couple of paracetamols were needed.'

'I've got some here,' Katie told her. 'Although the diagnosis is a bump on the head, not a night on the drink, and your sister here will confirm that.'

'I'm not her sister,' I said moving back and feeling overwhelmed by the situation.

'What do you mean not my sister?' She murmured with a weak smile before asking what she'd done to piss me off this time. As she leaned over to look at me she got a glimpse at my lower half and she screamed and put her hand over her face so that I couldn't see her crying, 'Oh

God, no, no, not this dream.'

'You're not dreaming,' I told her forcefully. 'If anyone's dreaming it's me, because you're dead.'

'No,' She replied 'You're dead and it's my fault and every night I see you in my dreams, wishing forever that I could reverse time and get my sister back but it can't happen. You're a ghost. I love you, but you have to stop haunting me. My therapist says these dreams are me lying to myself, because I want you to be alive, even if you're crippled, but you're not, you're dead. Please stop haunting me and be at peace in heaven….. Please.'

I sat back for a moment in shock. I remembered her face from the last time I saw it. I had never remembered anything about the car accident before, but seeing her in front of me brought it all back. It was a dream, obviously, but even though I was dreaming, there was a sudden moment when she stopped struggling and her eyes looked full of emotion, it took me back.

Drifting back over the years, something locked away deep in my memory took me back to the time my mind had been hiding from me so well for the last few years. I was in the most horrific pain. My head was bleeding, legs crushed under the steering column of my dad's Aston Martin. Maggy Grace was also trapped.

Despite the pain, I tried to look around and saw in the back of the car my little brother hanging limp. On the bonnet of our car was a limousine. We had hit it from behind on a mountain road and ploughed through the barriers, down the side of the mountain.

Our parents were in the car in front with our grandparents. I didn't remember how I hit their car up the arse, or what caused them to stop in front of me. The main thing that came back to me then, was my sister in the passenger seat, looking back at me as blood poured from her chest and legs. I remember nothing of her personality before those seconds when she stared at me with a tear forming in the corner of her eye. I wasn't sure if the look was a look of sisterly love, or one of accusation in knowing that my driving had just killed her.

She tried to open her mouth to talk, but she was too weak and so was I. The look was in her eyes for a second, and then everything went blank once more.

It must be a nightmare, that was it. I must have fallen asleep on the train. My greatest nightmares are two things, and they include losing any of my new friends I've made through work and having to face the ghosts of my dead family. That was it. I'd fallen asleep on the train because I was tired and ill and if I closed my eyes I would wake up and I'd be back on the train home.

I tried to close my eyes, but when I did all I saw was black, and when I opened them again I was still in the tent with Katie and the girl in the bed. It must have been a really strong nightmare brought on by meeting that freaky girl. She could have made me have this dream. Was it me wanting her to read me that had opened this whole can of worms in my head?

If I couldn't wake myself, then the best thing to do in this dream was walk away from the upset. As Katie stood over the girl trying to calm her down, I pushed myself back towards the bed where my crutches were propped up and re-attached my remaining leg.

I was about to pull myself into a standing position when Katie turned to me, pointing her finger and gave me the kind of look that says, 'What are you like, woman?' before grabbing my shoulders and putting me on the bed, saying, 'And where do you think you're going, young lady?' 'This isn't real it's just a dream.' I told her.

Katie looked at me like I was mad, and told me to remember that I'd just bumped my head. I retorted asking her if in her short time as a nurse, she had ever seen a bumped head bring a person back from the dead.

'She's right,' came a moan from the bed. 'It's a dream. I have them every night. She's always in my dreams as though she's stuck here. She's a ghost who's stuck in my head and can't move on, when I just want her to be free.'

Katie looked exasperated from each of us to the other, saying that if we kept this up she was going to need another cigarette rather quickly.

'Look, if anyone's dreaming or hallucinating it's me,' she told us, adding that as far as she was concerned, we were both alive and doing her nut in.

Both of us still refused to believe that the other was alive. Katie insisted that we needed to both stay there, saying she was sure we would believe differently when we were a bit more with it.

'But I saw my friend get taken by a monster and I need to go and help her.' I protested.

'You'll stay here until I say otherwise.' Katie snapped saying the last thing she needed if there were more casualties was either of us running away.

'I don't think I'll be 'running away' any time soon.' I giggled nodding at my crutches and my stumps.

'She can float away if she wants, seeing as she's a ghost.' The girl in the bed told us, turning away as though she was going back to sleep.

'Look, guys, there are no such things as ghosts, honestly, and nobody here is one.' Katie breathed looking like she was struggling to keep her cool. 'Calm,' she said, 'Sisters, not ghosts, sisters. I'm sure you love each other really.'

'I do love my sister,' the girl said, 'That's why I want her to go away up to heaven and be at peace, instead of reminding me of what happened to her.'

'And what did happen to me?' I asked a bit sharply, wishing I'd wake from this dream.

'Ladies, *calm,*' Katie bellowed, 'Take a step back here. While I'm here, nobody is going anywhere to look for anyone. Now...' she said once she had quiet. 'My mother has gone to the train to help the injured. She's a nurse and there are others who can help. I'm pretty sure that the people there will already have gone to get what help they can for the injured. Both of you seem to be in shock,' she shivered, walking over to a table which had on it a gas stove and a kettle. 'The treatment for shock...' she continued, clicking her lighter to light the hob. '...is to put your feet up with a nice warm caffeine-free beverage.'

'That's not going to happen,' I said bluntly, trying not to laugh at the flaw in this plan of Katie's to get us to put our feet up with a hot drink. The girl in the bed exchanged looks with me and she stopped looking scared for a moment and nearly laughed.

'Am I missing a joke?' Katie smiled kindly as she grabbed three cups from a rack beside the stove.

The girl in the bed gave me a mischievous look as she sat up and said to Katie, 'Don't worry, we're just putting our feet up.'

'Good, well done, ladies. Thanks for your cooperation, and...' She paused and looked me up and down. 'You can't put your feet up because you haven't got any.' 'I must have misplaced them.' I grinned.

My theory on my disability has always been to laugh because if you don't laugh, you cry. In fact, nowadays, with the popularity of the TV show 'Family Guy', a lot of my friends have started calling me Joe. This is in reference to the fact that I refuse to accept my disability. I work on the abilities I have, to make up for the ones I don't have.

The girl in the bed sat up and smiled at me. 'You look like my twin sister,' she smiled.

'And you look like my twin sister too,' I told her, shakily adding that I guessed her sister probably had legs. She nodded taking a sip of water with the paracetamol Katie had given her.

'I don't get this at all,' Katie said to us as she passed us both cups of cocoa, before sitting on the bed next to me.

The kettle must already have been warm when she put it on. 'You ladies don't know each other?' She asked and we both shook our heads. 'You have the same second name?' She continued, 'And...' she said to the other girl, '...You've got a picture of the pair of you together in your wallet.'

The pair of us looked at each other and spoke in unison, saying, 'But she *can't* be my sister.' We both paused to wait for the other to finish but then ended up speaking together once more. 'Because I killed my sister in a car accident.'

We sat for a moment, looking at each other without words, while Katie opened her pocket and took out one of her cigarettes and inspected it. When we asked what she was doing, she laughed and told us she was making sure she hadn't accidentally smoked her mum's weed.

Again, there was silence until Katie looked at us both and said, 'Okay, ladies, we need to make some sense of what's going on here. You're both going to tell me how you got to be out here.'

The girl looked at me in a manner which suggested she wanted me to go first. So, I told them what I remembered of how I got to be out in the field. However, for the sanity of any readers I'm not going to repeat it.

I included what happened in the build-up to the train coming off the rails and added in a few of the people I worked with, but I did not go as far as to tell them about my encounter with Jenny, in case it opened up the whole confusion of the girl being my sister.

They both sat there calmly listening to me until I finished and then the girl said to me gently, 'You really saw a monster take your friend?' I nodded and blew my nose gently.

She sat for a moment nodding to herself, drinking her cocoa, then she wiped her nose and gave me the most uneasy smile I had ever seen before telling us. 'I was on the train. I work for a company called Jessica's Enterprises. It's not called J&M, just J Enterprises. My boss is also called Jessica obviously. Mandy works for the company, but isn't in charge.'

I just sat there with my mouth open as she told me this, as did Katie.

'I believe you about the monsters too,' she said slowly looking from me to Katie who was staring at her with frightened eyes.

'Stop it,' Katie squealed, 'You two, this pretending not to know each other bullshit is scaring me.'

The girl, however, nervously shaking as she sipped her cocoa continued, picking up the wallet from the bed and looking at it as she spoke. 'It was a joke we used to play on people,' She mumbled. 'Me and my sister swapping identification so that nobody could tell us apart. I thought if I carried on the joke after she died, part of her would still be here. It's what she would have wanted, she would have found it funny.'

I think you may know where this is leading, depending on where my story is placed in the final edit of the book.

She sat and stared for a while, saying it couldn't be possible and it was all some fucked-up dream, but then she summed up the courage to look me dead in the eye, and she said, 'That's why I lie to everyone telling them I'm Maggy Grace Aricot when I'm Mary Georgina Aricot.

There was a stunned silence that seemed to last hours, even though it may well have only been minutes.

When I spoke, I tried to talk about the accident and ignore what the girl said, in favour of talking about what may be happening to my friends—remember I did not know at this point how many of my friends were safe. As far as I was aware, Jessie and Charlie had not made it off the train.

It was Katie who steered the conversation back to what the girl had said about her being me, to which we agreed that she must have hit her head very hard.

'It's very unlikely I agree,' she said quietly. '...but I swear on the life of everyone I know that I'm telling the truth.'

'But you can't be me, because, no offence, but I'm me.'

Katie was looking quite scared at us both. 'Is nobody even slightly freaked out by the fact you girls seemed to have the same story, and claim not to know each other.' 'I'm not, the girl claiming to be me frowned.

'You're not?' I asked, returning the frown.

Shrugging her shoulders she proceeded to tell us it all made perfect sense because both Katie and I were both in her imagination.

'You're my dead sister,' She smiled dreamily, 'But, my mind likes to make up these dreams that you are still alive, because that's where I want you to be, like the crash never happened,'

'How do you explain the lack of legs?'

She took a deep breath through her fingers, like a smoker who's subconsciously wishing they had a cigarette in their mouth when they don't have one, then she exhaled and replied. 'Sometimes in the dreams the crash happens, but you don't die like in real life. You lived with horrible injuries, but you lived on and didn't let it stop you, but still, I feel guilty for causing the crash.'

I tried to assure her it was okay by giving the usual line about she shouldn't worry about my legs, because you can't miss having a limb that you can't remember.

Chapter 11 Sharon

Rob told the story in Part One. I'm afraid it's me this time. I had a reputation in the group as a person who used their sex appeal to sell insurance. Some of the rumours even said that I was actually having sex with customers in return for sales. It was a joke started by me, to make myself come across a bit more interesting than your average thirty-something with personal issues. I like to think my customers had a little more class than sleeping with someone to seal the deal. I do admit to being a bit full-on and flirting, pulling my skirt up and wearing low-cut tops and that sort of thing, but nothing more. Plastering my face with make-up was not because I'm not pretty, but more because if I looked long enough at myself in the mirror I could pretend it was somebody else.

Amber was missing and that was all that mattered. Of course, Jack, Georgie and John mattered too, but Amber was my flatmate, so she was the one I was thinking of most. This whole mother-daughter pretence that went on between us was what kept me going.

I spent time in and out of care as a teenager and when I was about fifteen, I was abused by a man who got me pregnant. Because of my circumstances, my daughter was taken from me and her name was changed. I didn't even know where she was or if she even knew.

It was fitting that Amber was looking for her real mother at the same time that I was looking for my daughter. I tried to look after Amber, because she was the same age as my daughter, and I hoped somebody was looking after my girl in the same way.

I'm not in any way saying that I was any kind of role model for a teenager with my drinking and smoking. I must say, however, that t when Amber moved in with me, she already drank like a fish and smoked a pack a day. I was proud of her when she gave up her habits and took up exercising in search of answers to her health problems. I'm ashamed to say I did nothing to help her as I continued to smoke and drink around her.

I wanted to think that if that was my daughter out there in the dark for whatever reason they had all disappeared, then I would hope somebody was looking for her and keeping her safe. In a way, I hoped secretly that Amber never found her mum, just like I was never going to find my daughter. That way I could go on pretending she was my girl.

The reason I didn't talk so much to Rob before that night is that I was shy. Remember he said he was in a band called 'Rock Corn Storm, and nobody remembered them. That's not true. The band was from Colchester', but I was there at the waterfront in Norwich in their early gigs. In 1988 I even saved up all my cash to get a ticket for Queen: at Wembley Arena when I heard Rock Corn Storm would be opening for them. When a girl's favourite band splits, it's like the end of a passage in your life (Remember when take that split up) and it was sad seeing my hero, Rob Barn, ten years on in such a sad state that he didn't even play that bass I loved anymore. He didn't even recognise his number

one fan who was in the front row of every show.

So, who would have thought all these years on I'd be lost in the dark with Rob Barn? Who I was with, however, was the least of my worries when there were people in masks surrounding us in the dark as we lay on the floor in the mud.

They were terrifying. Not all of them wore masks, some of them had their faces painted with stripes and lines in colours ranging from black to gold and silver. The four of us, Rob, Greg, Mike, and myself, all stood up with our backs to each other in a defensive position as one of the masked figures stepped forward bearing both a flame torch and a long knife.

'State your intention,' he said, pointing the knife at Greg.

Greg froze for a second and looked at us with fear in his eyes, and said, 'Our train crashed and we're looking for some people.' He stopped and breathed hard, before continuing, 'Two guys and two girls, one of the girls has no legs.'

The man looked at him for a moment and then lowered the knife and the flame.

'There are strange and dangerous people out here tonight,' He said turning as though he meant us to follow.

Mike looked at Rob and then at me. 'He's in a dark field holding fire and a big knife, wearing a dress and makeup, and he tells us there are dangerous people out here?' He said quietly.

'Don't be scared of us,' said a soft female voice.

'Oh yeah,' Greg said not even bothering to hide his sarcasm. 'People point knives at me and you say don't be scared.'

'We didn't know who you were,' She said awkwardly.

'Well, we hardly know who you are either,' I breathed.

'Sharon Carter!' She said suddenly.

I stopped dead. Who? What? This person knew me? She paused for a second and removed her mask and I looked her up and down. 'Nicola Conway'

I gasped and then we both said together. 'What the hell are you doing out here?'

Nicola Conway was another victim of the UK care system. We were both troubled kids in and out of care and had gone to the same schools. We'd lost touch in more recent years. This was something that was easy to do at the time, remember Facebook was not invented for another four years.

'Like Greg said,' I told her, 'Our train crashed and we're looking for our friends.'

'Well don't be scared of us,' she laughed hesitantly, 'We might look scary, but we're pagans and we're friendly.'

'What exactly are you doing out here in a field in the middle of the night?' was Greg's retort.

'Leave it, Greg, they're friendly. That's all that matters right now.' Rob told him firmly.

'It's okay, it's Yule,' she told us

'Isn't a Yule log what we eat around Christmas?' Rob asked her hesitantly.

'Yes, but Yule has nothing to do with Christmas and it's a much older tradition,' another voice said from within the group.

'On the winter solstice, the shortest day of the year, we all come out here and pray to the goddess, and perform a spell to ask her to bring back the sun, so that spring can begin.'

'Basically, we all get dressed up and have a campfire and a few drinks and cheat on our partners.' Nicola told us with a smile. 'Scratch the last bit, well some do.' She added looking guilty.

'So why did that man pull a knife on Greg?' Rob demanded with a touch of anger in his voice.

'It's not just us out here,' she said breathlessly. 'We thought we'd be the only ones out here, but there's some big camp going on just out of sight from here and the

people there are like…'

'Like what?' I asked puzzled.

'I don't know how to explain it,' she replied, 'When we got here they came and warned us to stay away from the place and they were even weirder and scarier than us.'

'That's very difficult being weirder and scarier than people in masks pointing knives at people.'

'So, great, there are weird people out here in the field, but how does that help us find our friends?' Mike probed.

'We saw the train crash,' She said bluntly.

'We think those people at the camp might have had something to do with the crash, so we came to find them,' Said another woman, adding that a second group of people had gone to the train to see if they could help.

'Where are you taking us then?' I asked.

'To our first aid tent,' she replied.

'But none of us is hurt' Greg replied.

'We found two women laying in the field injured, and we need to know who they are' said the voice of the man who had threatened Greg, adding that one of them was missing both her legs.

'Georgie,' I breathed, hoping and praying that the other one was Amber.

He explained that they were both unconscious and receiving medical attention from a trainee nurse.

'Why did you think the other people caused the train crash?' Rob demanded changing the subject.

'We've seen them watching the railway all evening,' Nicola replied. 'There's something not right about them, they're terrifying, and they wear masks and dress all in black.'

'Oh, really just like you then,' Greg spat.

'They might dress like us and carry torches, and they may have come to worship the moon like us, but they're not like us.' Nicola said urgently adding, 'What we need to do is find your friends and get out of here.'

'I'm guessing you guys have cars somewhere,' I heard Greg ask more positively.

She shook her head. 'A few people came in cars and left them parked on a field in Halvigate but that's miles away. Most of us came in on the train after work this afternoon and walked from Berney Arms station on the other railway.'

'But some of you have cars within walking distance, so we can get help for our friends?' I asked and Nicola nodded.

'We sent two of our group back to their cars to go and call the police, knowing there was no phone signal here,' one of them replied.

'Those other people are part of your group too, right?' Mike asked sounding nervous. Several people stopped and looked around asking which other people Mike was talking about.

He was right. To our right-hand side, several balls of light had appeared, and they were coming at us rather quickly. There were several huge shapes moving among them. Not knowing better, I would have said they were giants or monsters of some kind. Other people had obviously seen them too as there was panic amongst the group.

'We don't have anyone over twenty feet tall in our group,' someone shouted, but they were almost drowned out by the battle cry of what sounded like over a thousand people charging at us out of the darkness. It was no good trying to run, as there was nowhere to go, and despite this, we tried but the 30 or so of us were quickly caught by the masses, and all I remember was a sharp crack as somebody hit me over the head.

Chapter 12 Amber

So, before we wrote the first part of our story, I was the one who wanted to do this the least. I was unsure of how to say the things I wanted to say and I was unsure of what to leave in, or what to leave out. I explained about the fact that I wanted to kill myself, having just found out that I was infertile with little chance of ever being able to adopt a child. I felt that my life was over, but when the train crashed and we could have died, it showed me how lucky I was to be alive and have what I had even if it was not what I wanted.

While other people are planning to get together later in the year and write Part Two, I must admit that I haven't waited to start my second part. In fact, I'm writing this on the same day as I wrote the first part, although actually, it's technically not, because it's actually about two in the morning the following day from our first get-together. I worked behind the bar in the pub last night and should have gone to bed long ago. However, I got the bit between my teeth and couldn't stop thinking about writing Part Two and it's my night off tomorrow or today.

So, using my land ladies' privileges, I made myself a big cup of coffee and ran a computer lead out to the outside table so I can sit and watch the sunrise over the harbour as I write.

I copied this idea from a friend called Rob Brownlow who sat out here with his wife while writing their story. 'A Midwinter night's dream.' I was enthralled by it and apparently, I did have a cameo role in the story, but I was the victim of a late edit due to my part being irrelevant to the story.

Back to our story. You may be surprised that I am still alive when you consider that my last entry finished with me being grabbed by a monster which came out of the darkness. Georgie confirms this.

So, as you can imagine, excuse my language, but I was so fucking terrified I couldn't breathe. Georgie says she tried to follow I have no reason to disbelieve her, but I couldn't see her even if she could see me. I was smoking so that probably made me easy to see in the dark. However, as the wind rushed by, I dropped my cigarette to the floor as I tried to scream without success. What in the hell was so big that it could pick me up in the way that it did? And what's more why? Why did something this big exist, and yet nobody knew about it?

Several thoughts ran through my head. It felt like there was a large ape-like hand holding me tight in its grip. Had I just been grabbed by King Kong? Or what if aliens had landed and that was what caused the train to derail, and they'd got me and maybe they were going to put a probe up my bum? But then why would they choose me? Surely there were better bottoms to put probes up than mine.

I shouldn't make a joke of it, and I can tell you I was so scared I'll honestly tell you, I well and truly wet my knickers. Whatever the creature was, it ran for at least two minutes before it began to slow.

Finally, just as I found my voice and began to scream it suddenly stopped running, then there was a crunching noise as if something was being up-rooted from the ground. The creature dropped me on the marsh where I fell breathlessly, my heart pounding. Before I had the chance to move, there was another big thump and the ground shook again.

As I stood up and tried to run for my life, I ran straight into a brick wall. What in the hell was a brick wall doing out in the middle of the marshes? My first thought was to feel my way around it. However, it seemed to be a wall around me. How was there suddenly a wall around me?

'Help,' I screamed into the darkness, but my screams just came back off of the wall.

'Be quiet child,' came a thick voice from the other side of the wall. Fright ran down my tingling spine like a drip from an icicle.

'Be careful there's a monster!' I warned.

'Shhh, child,' the voice told me. 'It's rude to call somebody who's saved you a monster.'

'What?' I said out loud. It was the monster itself that was talking to me, but how? 'How are you speaking to me?' I called.

'In English, you silly blonde,' it replied.

'But how did you save me when I was perfectly okay?' I asked, adding that I got off the train when it crashed and some of my friends were dead and I hardly needed saving after the event.

'I wasn't saving you from the train,' the voice groaned, 'I was saving you from the things that caused the train to crash.'

'I don't believe you. You've brought me here to play with me before you eat me or stick a probe up my bum!'

'Sophie, I might be a monster, but I'm not an alien, and I am not going to eat you.' The voice said in an urgent, but hushed tone.

I tried to think of a retort, but suddenly my mouth dropped open. 'Y-you know m-my n-name!' I stuttered. 'How do you know my name?' I must add that for those of you who may have forgotten, I did explain in Part One that my real name is Sophie, and that Amber is a name of my own making.

'Sophie Spellman,' it said in a softer tone. 'as a child when your mother chased you, you would run off into the forest at the back of the house and hide in a tree, sobbing, before running to the boy who lived on the other side of the wood.'

How could this beast hiding in the dark have known these things? When I asked in a panic the creature replied, 'There are many things the human race sees, but pretends it doesn't because it is scared of the truth.'

'That's true,' I replied, 'But that doesn't explain who or what you are, or how you know me,' I yelled in the direction of where I thought it was.

I was terrified on so many levels, although this thing said it was here to save me. One, I was scared shitless that many of my friends were dead. Two, how on earth had people missed the fact that there was a giant ape running around the countryside?

Three, there was a giant ape running around the countryside and four, it knew all about me. I spent a lot of my youth hiding in the woods at the back of my parents' garden. I would climb trees so that I knew they couldn't follow me. I often climbed a tree and had a good cry when my adopted mother beat me up. From the age of about twelve, I started stealing alcohol and cigarettes from the village shop and taking them into the forest to consume. Jack always knew where to find me and he would usually be the one to snatch the alcohol and fags from me and hide with me until I'd sobered up.

'One day when you were ten years old, you misbehaved yourself at school and your stepmother was called,' The creature breathed, 'That evil woman took you home, but before she could beat you, you escaped out of the car and ran for the trees, but as you climbed higher, the branch broke and you fell.'

I remembered everything he said. Janette Brownlow and Donna Fox from the school year above me were teasing me. I overreacted and punched both of them. That wasn't a good thing to do when Donna's mother was the headmistress. I will say that I don't wish to speak any further ill of either of the girls, because I later made my peace with both ladies as well as Mrs Fox. Tragically, Mrs Fox took her own life some years ago, her daughter Donna went missing not long after, and has to my knowledge never been found. Janette was the older sister of my friend Rob Brownlow whom I mentioned earlier. She died in a plane crash in 2008 along with her four-year-old daughter, and her whole family apart from her little brother.

Back to that day, I remembered my mum was in a terrifying rage and to avoid the beating I ran out of the car and jumped the fence, running with all the energy I had until I reached the tallest tree I could find and tried to climb, but I was climbing too fast when the branch broke and I fell.

As I fell, I had thought that I would surely die, but somehow something had broken my fall. That was where I had seen the monster before. It was he who had caught me. I'd looked up into his eyes too scared to scream at the ugliest, yet kindest thing I had ever seen in my whole life. He wasn't an ape, he was tall and scaled, with big claws and pointy ears and a long nose. He didn't look like the troll from the illustrated storybook of the Three Billy Goats Gruff, he was much bigger and much scarier, yet he saved me. Before I could say a word, he just gave me a look all over and left me there speechless.

I had always thought that I hit my head really hard and my mind made it all up. 'That's it, isn't it?' I said out loud. 'I hit my head on the train and now I'm seeing things.'

'My name is Ulskain, and I am a battle troll,' he breathed.

'Well, what's a battle troll? and what were you doing in the woods all those years ago? What are you doing here? And why have you trapped me?'

He was silent for a while before speaking, but nothing he said made any sense to me, but then nothing made sense anymore with monsters running about the place.

'My colony lives in the village of Norringsham where you were born and we are under the command of the Red Witch.' He grunted.

'Who in God's name is the Red witch? And what in the great big fuck-balls of hell has it got to do with me or my friends...? And...' I added, 'If you work for a Red-headed witch, she sounds really bad.'

'It's got nothing to do with your friends,' he said gruffly, adding, 'But, they are all in grave danger.

'The Red-headed Witch is a child who has not yet gained her powers and she is under my protection and currently has no knowledge of her destiny,' he said in an attempt at a whisper. As you can understand I wasn't even sure if I was dreaming as this was all so absurd, but I thought I'd better ask exactly why he had kidnapped me if he was supposed to be protecting this so-called child witch.

'The child I protect is safe as long as the bad people are here, then she is in no danger. You, on the other hand, were just involved in a train crash and now you're in mortal peril.'

'But why am I any more worth saving than the others? And how am I in mortal peril now I'm off of the train?' I pressed bewildered and even more intrigued by his reply.

'My colony has no interest in fighting,' he grunted, 'However, in my duty to keep the peace, I infiltrated the battle trolls who take their orders from those who seek to destroy the earth, and they believe me to be among their ranks.'

'Okay... but what does this have to do with me? Is it to do with when I was a child?'

'It is in part, but it's also a coincidence,' he said trying to speak quietly.

I felt in my pocket for my lighter and clicked it, and a ball of light erupted showing me that I was inside some kind of circular wall.

'There's no time to explain all,' he said hurriedly. '...but there is more to this world than you will ever know, and there is an uprising about to take place on this marshland this night. There are groups of magical forces—one good, one bad that have been fighting over the human race for centuries. One using magic to protect humans from the other, which used magic to kill. It all came to a head when I was a child in the late 1600s when two dying warriors saved the planet with a charm which was to stop the bad side using their powers to kill humans.'

'Alright, whatever!' I said impatiently, looking for a way out of my prison. This horrible experience was obviously a dream. That was it. There was no train crash. I was in bed dreaming all of the bad stuff that had happened. Who knows perhaps the train crash was not real and I would wake up and find that the appointment with my consultant that morning—the one where he told me I would never have children—was not real either.

'Stop talking this shit about magic and witches,' I said impatiently. 'Trolls don't belong here. You belong under bridges in fairy tales.'

I heard him sigh. 'Must that tale stick with my kind for the rest of eternity?'

'Well,' I said flashing my light around the place, looking for a door or a place to climb. 'When you read it in a book from a young age, you tend to associate trolls with

goats and bridges, but I'd love to know how you'd fit under a bridge.'

'That troll was my aunty,' he said quietly.

'It was a man in every version I read,' I scoffed, and I swear I heard him reply something about his aunt having a beard.

Suddenly, I saw a door right behind where I stood. I had to get back to my friends, however, I stopped, still terrified that if I got out he would do something to hurt me.

'Look...' he said grumpily. '...whether or not you choose to believe me about the magic, which I find it hard to believe you wouldn't, seeing as you're talking to a giant troll. You must believe me, I've shut you in this place for your own protection.'

'Alright?' I called up into the night stepping away from the door, 'But if these people are so dangerous, why are you only protecting *me* when all my friends were left out there to be killed?'

I felt a little bad when he answered that, like me, he only had two hands and couldn't save everyone.

'So, why is it so important that these people don't get me?' I pleaded to know. 'Please don't tell me you rescued me, because you felt you knew me.'

'Tonight is a blood moon,' he growled as quietly as he could. 'The servants of Satan believe that in this place on the winter solstice, combined with the power of the moon, they can summon a force of power like the world has not seen in a thousand years. They're hoping the power will break the charm that prevents them from using their magic to kill humans.'

'Okay, say for one moment this is not a dream and that I do believe you,' I squealed, trying to stall him as I leaned against the door which was made of rotten wood, trying to break it so I could make a run for it. 'If these people are aiming to eradicate us humans, but they can't use magic and they have an army of trolls like you, why don't they just get the trolls to stamp on everyone? Ha ha.' I thought I'd got him with that one.

'My colony would stand and fight them…' He stalled, 'but we are few in number and hunted to near extinction with a huge loss of habitat and hiding places. The devil worshipers only have ten trolls in this country, while those of us still loyal to the protectors have only seven. But if they came out in the open, the army would bomb the shit out of them, and then there would be none. However, if the charm is broken, then creatures of all shapes and sizes will come from the shadows, and the forces of evil will be unopposed to wipe the earth clean.'

'So,' I said, pushing hard on the door. 'Why do you need to keep me safe? Why am I special? Why not one of my friends?'

'Because, to break the charm they need to sacrifice two pure and innocent people.'

'Pure? Innocent? Me? Who the fuck are you kidding?' I nearly laughed.

'What's funny child?' he snarled.

'Well,' I replied sarcastically, taking a breather from my effort to break the door. 'I'm hardly pure and innocent. I smoke like a chimney, I drink until I'm blind drunk, I swear fuck knows how much, and I beat up friends when I get angry.'

'Your purity has nothing to do with addiction or choice of words,' he snarled, 'It's simply the fact that you have never mated with another human that makes you pure.'

My jaw dropped. 'What…? This is all because I'm a virgin and if they kill me it could end the world?'

'Two virgins are required, one female and one male,' he hissed. He must have been breathing towards the door because a spray of foul-smelling breath wafted through. 'They have the man, but as long as I have you hidden away here, they can't perform the sacrifice.'

'You fucking moron,' I yelled. If they are killing virgins out there, then locking me in here isn't going to help a great deal when they just pick up the next one and use her. If what this crazy monster was saying was true, I didn't want to think of any of the other virgin women in our group being burned alive, or some horrible shit like that.

'You're the only female in your party who has never mated,' He growled. 'How do you know who's a virgin and who isn't' I demanded. 'Do you go around checking in people's bedroom windows all night like a dirty creep?'' It's a smell,' he boomed, 'Every person who has mated has a smell that humans cannot detect, and you are the only female in the group not to have that smell and that male you hung around with as a child doesn't have it either and that's why they took him.'

I was exhausted from trying to break the door and for a moment my pounding heart stopped. When he told me, they had a male virgin I thought he was talking about Gregory. My mind was overloaded with things, this had to be a dream, the likelihood of there being trolls and witches was very small, but the likelihood that anyone had ever had sex with Gregory was unthinkable.

Jack, he lied to me, when I was trying to push him away. Don't get me wrong I loved Jack and that's why I wanted him to see other girls. I wanted him to be happy when I couldn't make him. He assured me that although he was single now he had done the deed on more than one occasion. However, it seemed he was lying to keep me happy and now if this was real, he was in mortal peril.

Knowing Jack needed my help I smashed at the door with all I was worth and somehow it came crashing down.

The instant I was out of the door, the troll grabbed me in a massive hand and roared. 'For the sake of this earth, you are going nowhere.'

Chapter 14 Sharon

I woke up, everything was blurred, my body was hurting all over and I was incredibly hot. This seemed to be because there was a very big fire burning very close to me. As my sight improved, I could see many small groups of people sat in the light of the fire, all of them in groups of four sitting back to back with their legs out straight. I tried to stand, but found myself seemingly tied to the people behind me although I couldn't see a rope of any sort. I felt sick as a dog as I looked around, there were a lot of people who I didn't recognise and many I did.

Searching the faces, I saw James, Chris, Carol, Rachel, and Ben. Over my left there and then my heart skipped a beat as I saw Amber and Jack. Amber caught my eye and I tried to stand up to run over and hug her, but I seemed to be stuck fast to the people around me. I managed to twist my head around far enough to see that the person my back was against was Rob. Nicola was in floods of tears on my right-hand side and to my left was the man who had put the knife to Gregg's throat.

Amber was beaten black and blue, and there was a tear of sorrow and distress in her eye as she looked at me, and said loudly and clearly, 'I love you, Mum and Dad.'

It must have been the madness of the utterly appalling situation we found ourselves in. Or maybe Amber was just being nice in showing that she thought of me as her mum. If that was the case, who on earth was she referring to as her dad because the only person I could see her looking at was Rob and I might well have been his biggest fan and fancied the pants off of him, but I never dated him.

I'd always known there was a possibility that Amber was my daughter who was taken from me when I was fifteen but I never told her because I knew she would think badly of me. Whatever was going on, I needed to talk to her about it in case it was the last chance I got. Even if it was in front of a hundred people I needed this talk with her.

'When did you find out?' I asked.

She looked bewildered as she replied, 'Find out what?'

'That I'm your mother,' again she looked utterly perplexed as she tried to shrug her shoulders.

'What do you mean?' She asked, now looking around at all the people who had stopped trying to break free of whatever the force was that seemed to be holding people together.

'How long have you known I was your mother?'

It was Jack who answered the question rather than Amber this time saying, 'You've been her mother as long as I've known her and that's a long time.'

I must have hit my head really hard and still not be with it because this wasn't real.

Amber smiled and said, 'Best mum in the world!' then she looked at Rob and said, 'Best dad too'.

Rob must have looked equally perplexed because Amber continued saying 'I know you marrying my mum when I was 10 years old hardly makes you my real dad but you're the best step-dad ever.'

'I have no idea what you're talking about' Rob told her, adding that we should all be trying to figure out a way of getting out of this situation.

'I do agree there.' She smiled with more tears falling down her face. 'It's just with all this shit going on I'm pretty sure we're going to die in this freaky place with these people. I just wanted to say it was a pleasure to have you as parents' Then she paused and looked at Jack and 'to have the best husband in the world.

I choked so loudly that everyone looked around from her to me. 'B-but when on earth did you guys get married?' I babbled.

'What do you mean mum? You were there last April. You said I was crazy getting married at 16 but you gave your blessing and Dad you walked me down the aisle.' She was looking at Rob.

'Amber I must have amnesia,' he replied quietly, 'because I don't remember even being with Sharon let alone marrying her.' 'No offence Sharon' He added quickly before stating he was as shocked as anyone that Amber was my daughter.'

'But you walked me down the aisle, Dad,' she protested, 'And what is this Amber thing about?'

'What do you mean, it's your name,' I replied to her bluntly.

'No, it isn't' She retorted 'My name is Sophie, I was born Sophie Carter, then when you married Dad I was Sophie Barn, then I married Jack and now I'm Sophie Ram.'

She looked very hurt and upset at the fact that we all looked so shocked by this revelation.

There wasn't any time to dwell on what was said because a woman had entered the light in front of us. She was in her mid to late Twenties and looked a bit like……. Well to be brutally honest she looked a bit like me.

She was blonde and plastic-like, her face was covered in make-up as though she thought it made her look pretty but it actually rather detracted from her looks. I'm fully aware that my own addiction to make-up and perfume is just as bad. She looked like she had just got there from work and was still wearing what looked like a hotel receptionist uniform.

Her voice was amplified through some sort of sound system, 'Oh, hi my lovelies,' she said in a voice that sounded as though she was greeting friends in a false and overly sweetened tone. There was a chorus of shouts from all sides asking for help to get free. She gently waved away each person pushing her hands down asking for silence and when she got it she spoke.

'Good evening everyone,' she said in her overly sweetened voice with a beaming smile, 'My name is Katherine (call me Kathy) and tonight you, my sweeties will be given a task.' 'What task?' Someone asked, 'All in good time' she replied.

'As you will see you have been magically bound together. My magical friends and I are creating a new world here tonight and we require two virgins, we have a boy. Unfortunately, you have all been checked. None are suitable apart from a girl who has regrettably escaped. Her name is Amber Spellman and for every 5 minutes I don't have her, one of you will die.'

She looked around for someone to give her an answer but there were no takers. There were cries of 'What's going on?' and 'Let us go please'

'What are you like my darlings? It's not very nice not to answer my question is it my cherubs,' she leaned around the room with a frog like smile.

'Well, you're all going to die at some point this evening so the person who tells me where she is first can die last!'

She beamed her frog like smile one more time clapping her hands and said sweetly, 'Chop chop my lovelies.'

We all looked at each other panicked for both ourselves and Amber. Mike looked around at us in desperation and shouted to her. 'We don't know where she is and wouldn't tell if.......'

He didn't get to finish his sentence. Somebody had run out of the shadows so quickly we didn't see them and before they retreated, they had cut Mike's throat. All that he made was a gurgling sound as blood poured out of him. Within seconds he had died right there in front of us. You could hear a pin drop amongst the crowd.

'Oops, poor dearie' The woman, Katherine said pulling a mock face of concern. 'His mother should have told him it was rude to interrupt. I trust none of you will be so silly now you know I mean business. You have 4 minutes and 32 seconds until another one dies.'

Derailed and Dispersed Volume 3 is out now

Derailed and dispersed in volume 3, the sacrifice of virgins is out now. To purchase your copy please go to Amazon. For a signed copy please email Samwhite@gmail.com

Printed in Great Britain
by Amazon